'Teenagers *is a bold and practical app* wisdom to twenty-first-century parentir *away from God's unchanging standards,* .... *does she allow the reader to feel guilty or inadequate.* Teenagers *blends responsibility with redemption in this sympathetic yet challenging call to relational, hands-on parenting.'*

Revd Richard Cunningham, Director of UCCF: The
Christian Unions, husband of Ruth and father of five

'*We have rarely seen the book of Proverbs so helpfully applied. Here is wise counsel for dealing with the best and worst of teenage life. Completely contemporary and thoroughly biblical family advice!'*

Revd Stephen and Janet Gaukroger,
Clarion Trust International

'*Here is a book that is honest and practical, offering help and wisdom for navigating your way successfully through the jungle of parenting teenagers. We wish we had read it years ago!'*

Revd Ian and Ruth Coffey, Moorlands College

Ann Benton

Biblical wisdom
for parents

ivp

INTER-VARSITY PRESS
Norton Street, Nottingham NG7 3HR, England
Email: ivp@ivpbooks.com
Website: www.ivpbooks.com

First published 2008

British Library Cataloguing in Publication Data
A catalogue record for this book is available from the British Library.

ISBN: 978-1-84474-354-4

Set in 12/15 pt Monotype Dante
Typeset in Great Britain by Servis Filmsetting Ltd, Stockport, Cheshire
Printed in Great Britain by Ashford Colour Press, Gosport, Hampshire

Inter-Varsity Press publishes Christian books that are true to the Bible and that communicate the gospel, develop discipleship and strengthen the church for its mission in the world.

Inter-Varsity Press is closely linked with the Universities and Colleges Christian Fellowship, a student movement connecting Christian Unions in universities and colleges throughout Great Britain, and a member movement of the International Fellowship of Evangelical Students. Website: *www.uccf.org.uk*

CONTENTS

ACKNOWLEDGMENTS

I must start by acknowledging my debt to the grace of Almighty God in my own life and in the lives of my children. It would be unforgivably smug and a downright travesty to write a book on parenting, presenting myself as the possessor of unique insights and an impeccable track record. You would only have to talk to my husband or children to expose that as fantasy.

On the contrary, I want to state at the outset that any wisdom I have is from God. Much of it came via the many mistakes I have made. That is why I have attempted to base this book on God's word alone and not on my ideas or experiences. The adventure of reading God's word is a daily pleasure which I commend to everyone. Its relevance to life here and now never ceases to amaze me. It can be truly said to give light to the eyes.

Secondly, I want to acknowledge the help of other people. Because my experience of raising teenagers has been limited to a mere four, I needed to consult others – parents, teachers, youth leaders – to get a broader picture. I am grateful to those who took time and trouble and some pain to recount their stories, particularly 'Andrew and Nicky' whose experiences informed a large part of chapter 7.

Thirdly, I am grateful to those who read this book (family, friends and strangers) in its various incarnations and fed back their comments and suggestions. Eleanor Trotter at IVP was gentle in her criticism and warm in her encouragement. I needed both.

Finally, I want to thank John, husband, lover, tea-maker, best friend and partner in child-rearing. What fun it has been! If I had to do it all over again, I would still want to do it with you.

PREFACE

What is this book about?

Our perception, that is, my husband's and my own, was that once our children began secondary school, the years gathered pace. Things were coming at us in quick succession, chiefly via interminable letters from the school, extracted from trouser pockets: assignments, coursework, opportunities, exams, events, trips, decisions, choices. Before we knew it, that skinny schoolboy with his blazer buttoned up and his brand new schoolbag was blocking the light when he entered the kitchen. He had a deep voice and a hint of stubble on his chin and he was talking about gap years and UCAS forms.

The intervening years were so hectic, it was hard at times to recall what we were supposed to be doing as parents. It is generally assumed that, above everything else, parents want their children to be happy. In addition, there is huge pressure that their children be successful, however you choose to measure that success. But is that all?

A father in the Bible set this priority before his (probably teenage) son: 'Above everything else, get wisdom.' Wisdom is commended as the key to health, happiness, prosperity and everything else you could desire. Your job as a parent is not first and foremost to make your children happy or successful, but to do what you can to make them wise.

This book is about teenagers and the pursuit of wisdom. What is wisdom? Why do teenagers need it? How are they to get it? And what about the parents of teenagers, who are frequently only too well aware that they need it too?

This book is written for parents at that stage. I hope they will read it before the onset of the teenage years and that it will help them to know what they are about and be prepared for what they might have to face.

It is intended primarily for parents who are Christian believers. I will be delighted if it is read by unbelievers and firmly adhere to the view that the Bible's truth is true for everybody, regardless of racial, cultural or religious background. In as far as this book gives advice, I intend that it will be useful to any parent. However, the assumptions behind that advice will unashamedly be those of a Christian worldview.

In my descriptions of the attitudes and behaviour of teenagers I have tried to be both realistic and biblical. The fact is, teenagers can be great and they can be awful. If you have only met the former kind, be thankful; if the latter, know that you are not alone. In our family at different seasons we had both kinds. However, the overall experience of parenting our four children through those teenage years was an education I would not have missed. Put simply, it was really nice having them around and watching them grow into people we now count as the best of friends.

Many parents acknowledge that they could use a little help and encouragement. It is my prayer that this book will offer just that.

Ann Benton
Guildford, June 2008

1. INTRODUCTION: THE SURVIVAL HANDBOOK

> *'There's that meeting on at church tonight,' said Kate to John over their macaroni cheese. 'You know, about parenting. Shirley phoned up to remind us.'*
>
> *'A bit late for all that, isn't it?' said John, staring at the empty third chair. 'Where is Daisy, anyway?'*
>
> *'There's some rock band on somewhere and she's gone with Jake and all that crowd.'*
>
> *John sighed his habitual sigh. 'I don't suppose we know when she'll be back.'*
>
> *After a pause, Kate said, 'We'll give that meeting a miss then, shall we?'*
>
> *'I think it will only make us feel bad,' agreed John.*

If you are into comic and ironic writing, you may have come across 'The Worst Case Scenario' series of handbooks. These are books which take a semi-humorous, somewhat quirky approach to handling the trials of life. They envisage a range of dreadful situations and give, with mock serious-ness and handy illustrations, step-by-step instructions on self-extrication/preservation. They are particularly suited to the kind of paranoid, obsessive people who always want to locate the fire exit door as soon as they enter a building.

In the survival handbook on parenthood in this series, there is a section on the teenage years. A brief glance at the subject headings indicates the kind of experiences and fears we are dealing with.

- How to tell if your child was switched at birth
- How to soundproof your teenager's room
- How to deal with provocative clothing
- How to bond with your teenager (helpful advice there about how to perform an 'ollie' on a skateboard and how to DJ a party)
- How to survive your child's first date
- How to survive your child's first driving lesson
- How to track your teenager's movements
- How to survive a meeting with the headteacher

If any of those headings resonate with you, you have a teenager. There are times when you look at the cute, cheru-bic three-year-old face grinning at you from the photo on the sideboard and wonder how that child turned into the sullen, gangling creature sprawled on the sofa. You wish you under-stood how they could possibly like the music they do; you can't believe they are going out looking like that; and you wish you knew not only what they are thinking, but also where they are. Perhaps there are times when, despite the assessment of your best friends that you are desperately in need of advice on parenting, like Kate and John, that is the very last thing that you feel you can face.

Kate's and John's negative response to the invitation is not unreasonable. Parents are understandably touchy about their children's progress and behaviour. Sometimes they cover this by talking up the measurable achievements and accredited activities. (Recall all those Christmas newsletters.) They have got the message that it is very important to be positive and encouraging. Occasionally this is at the expense of reality.

Other parents continually look over their shoulders and are privately wistful and disappointed with their progeny. Parenting is a competitive sport. From potty training to university entrance, no achievement is valued purely for what it is, but only if it stands out in comparison to the achievements of the offspring of 'friends', colleagues and associates. Peer group pressure is not confined to teenagers. So any parent of a child who is perceived as not making the accepted 'grade' hardly needs reminding of the fact. Such parents are already in sackcloth and ashes, although those garments may be hidden under a business suit.

Kate's and John's response raises another issue. Is there a point at which even the best of advice, humbly received, is pointless because it comes too late? The horse has not only bolted, but has been rounded up and dispatched at the knackers' yard. The stable and its door are obsolete. This is a serious and sensible question and one to which I shall return.

Are teenagers a subject of their own?

I have been giving talks on parenting for many years. And for many years I declined invitations to talk about teenagers. The main reason was that old joke about the car driver who stopped and asked a pedestrian the way to a particular place. The pedestrian shook his head, pursed his lips and said, 'Well,

I wouldn't start from here.' That is precisely the point when talking about parenting strategies for teenagers. You wouldn't start from there.

The patterns of years

The fact is, you haven't started from there. There is a history of upwards of a dozen years of input of some kind. Already that input will be yielding its own particular harvest. The rod of discipline (whatever you want to understand that to be) is at its most effective before the age of five. The warm relationship characterized by good communication, which is the necessary context for effective discipline, is a result of unstinting, unselfish effort over a long period of time. Such a thing is not developed with a thirteen-year-old in a day, or a week, or a month by following a five-point plan. The relationship you have with your teenage son, be it matey or hostile, is the result of years of habitual interaction. It is woven into the fabric of everyday relating, overlaid with years of collective memories, convenient routines and mutually accepted patterns of behaviour. Such patterns, even if deemed inappropriate or unhelpful, can be very hard to break. Like picking up dropped stitches in a complicated piece of knitting, it is not impossible, but it is tricky and painstaking work. That does not mean, of course, that the attempt should not be made. This book will argue that it should.

It needs to be remembered also that even the 'best' of parents of the 'best' of children will meet new challenges in the teenage years. Some of these challenges will take them by surprise. They thought they understood their child; they thought certain issues had been dealt with. They thought that sound early training would mean that their offspring would make sound choices. They do not know how to respond when the opposite turns out to be the case.

A *separate stage*

So, further consideration has led me to believe that there are good reasons for viewing the teenage years as a separate / transitional stage and one well worth examining on its own account. The obvious reason is that the children themselves during those years are undergoing huge physical and physiological changes. I am not a medic and I do not intend to talk about hormones in this book, but it does not take an expert to observe that growth and development between the ages of ten and twenty is rapid, extraordinary and sometimes temporarily unsightly. As James Dobson aptly puts it, as a chapter heading in *Preparing for Adolescence*, 'Something crazy is happening to my body!'

While the young teenager is trying to adjust to all of the crazy things that are happening to his or her body, the teenager's parent also has some adjustment to make, in perception, attitude and behaviour.

- In perception, because what you have developing, fuming or pouting in front of you is no longer a child. You are seeing the five-year-old, but the fifteen-year-old is a different beast.
- In attitude, because although he / she is still very much under your authority, that authority is waning and will ultimately (we hope and pray) become influence. When your child is small you tell him precisely what to do and when. You direct his time; you make choices for him from his clothing to his schooling. As he grows you are training him to make good choices for himself; by the time he is eighteen he is responsible for the choices he makes and the consequences of them. You are no longer laying out the sailor suit on his bed.

- In behaviour, because your teenager is not an adult, but neither is she a child. There is a vast difference between relating to a four-year-old and relating to a fourteen-year-old. The four-year-old will gladly walk along holding your hand; the fourteen-year-old will die if you even touch her in front of her friends.

When your child begins secondary school (which is a massive cultural change of its own requiring substantial adjustments), it would therefore seem to be a good time to do some appraisal of how your parenting work is going along and to take a look at what might be coming to meet you on the road ahead.

Where should we look for advice?

Although my university education was in the field of psychology, it is not from the thoughts and findings of psychological theorists or researchers that I shall be drawing my suggestions and conclusions. A crucial tenet of the Christian faith is that the God who made the universe and everything in it has revealed himself in the Bible. It is through a reading of the Bible that humans can understand the world they inhabit.

It has been said elsewhere that the Bible is not a collection of therapeutic insights. Those who try to use it in this way are on very thin ice. The Bible is one big story about how God made a people for himself, a people he singularly loved. Despite their ingratitude and rebellion, God persevered in executing a rescue plan to deliver them from the ruin they were bringing on themselves. The Bible tells how, as God worked in human history, he called, rescued, led, preserved and judged his people and ultimately was faithful, and continues to be faithful, to all the promises he made.

Kate and John, like all Christian parents, might be surprised and encouraged to be reminded of some key truths of Scripture and let the implications of those truths filter down to shape and reshape their attitudes and behaviour towards this loved but infuriating or incomprehensible member of the family, the teenager. That is what this book is about. I cannot promise that this book will always make you feel affirmed. It might sometimes make you feel guilty, but one of the truths of Scripture is that guilt can be good for you if you know what to do with it.

Somewhere near the middle of the Bible are the writings known as wisdom literature: Proverbs, Song of Songs, Ecclesiastes. These are a separate genre from the narrative and prophecy which make up most of the rest of the Old Testament. They are an insert into the main big story, revealing aspects of the way in which the world God has made works. Most of the Scripture references in this book are taken from the book of Proverbs. It might be stretching the point, but you could say that the Bible has its own survival handbook for parents and that handbook is the book of Proverbs. *This* book has come out of a reading and re-reading of *that* book.

Why Proverbs?

I chose the book of Proverbs as my basis, firstly because it makes no assumptions about the reader. These pithy sayings, collected together in what frequently seems a random way, can be applied indiscriminately. In contrast, some Christian writers and parents have wondered why their children lack Christian virtues, like patience, kindness, gentleness, meekness, goodness and self-control. They are keen to promote the growth of what are called in Galatians 5 'the fruit of the Spirit'. But the fruit of the Spirit grow where the Holy Spirit

Don't look to harvest tomatoes if tomato seeds were never sown.

has been at work. That might or might not be the case in our children. Don't look to harvest tomatoes if tomato seeds were never sown.

A game of two paths

On the other hand, the book of Proverbs has something to say to those whose children, from a human point of view, 'could go either way'. It is all about this, packed to the brim with the idea that life presents choices: this path and that path. The teenager's parent is very often, like the writers of Proverbs, in the position of watching, with bated breath or with tears, to see which path it will be.

Secondly, I chose Proverbs because much of it is written as advice from a parent to a child. The first nine chapters and much of the last eight are addressed to 'my son'. And since the subjects covered include much on the subject of controlling the sexual appetite, it is fair to assume that the intended addressee has reached, or nearly reached, puberty. Hence they are highly relevant to the clientele we have in mind.

Thirdly, Proverbs presents key truths of Scripture but from the point of view of one who watches the world and its inhabitants and reflects on what he sees from the evidence all around him. I imagine the writer looking from his window or standing by the city gate, observing the behaviour of the various characters who pass by: the fool, the sluggard, the nagging wife, the drunkard. Thus human depravity and accountability are here alongside God's sovereign purposes and love. There is human love and faithfulness as well as its opposite. There are failures and mistakes; there is redemption and hope; there is laughter and tears, all observed from the ground. This is real life in a fallen world, but one which has not been abandoned by its Creator.

A foundational truth

Let us, by way of example, begin with a foundational truth concerning the nature of a teenager.

You can go to Waterstone's and find a shelf full of books on parents and children. Many of them will contain helpful tips and advice, but few start from where the Bible starts, with an accurate description of where children are coming from.

> Folly is bound up in the heart of a child,
>> but the rod of discipline will drive it far from him.
> (Proverbs 22:15)

In one sentence we have the problem outlined, but we also have a solution prescribed.

The legendary waywardness of youth is not acquired via their iPod; it was already present when that teenager was in his baby buggy. Human beings from conception have a natural inclination towards selfishness and sin. This is a disease which children have in common with

The legendary waywardness of youth is not acquired via their iPod; it was already present when that teenager was in his baby buggy.

their parents. If parents and those who advise them would accept this fact, they would stop trying to excuse, blame or deny and would set about, from the earliest years, the task of training in obedience and setting sensible boundaries. Children do not learn to be naughty; their naughtiness is an expression of what they are: sinners. Folly is bound up in their hearts. The explanation of how this came about is found at the beginning of Genesis. Early on in the history of the human race, human beings made it clear to their Maker that they did not want to abide by their Maker's rules. Humans had ambitions to be god themselves and have ever since been congenitally incapable of recognizing that the role is too big for them. This is the inbuilt folly of the human race. We all share it. Original sin is a fact of life.

Even non-Christians are increasingly acknowledging the presence of original sin, if not by that name. The education-alist Sue Palmer has written a sensible and well-researched book entitled *Toxic Childhood*, examining all the aspects of contemporary life which make childhood not what it used to be and not what we would want it to be. She comments, 'In defending the culture we've created, we have to recognise that the barbarians are not only at the gate, they're in the womb.'

The Bible's view of human nature is realistic. If we embraced this view, perhaps we would be less shocked by the headlines about teenagers who bully, maim or stab others. All that has happened is that, just as with increasing years there is the move towards increased independence, the expression of that waywardness (which inhabits all of us) finds less acceptable, more shocking expression.

The untended human heart, according to the Bible, is an unexploded bomb. The proverb quoted above is making the observation that good training and consistent discipline, especially in the early years, are crucial to the raising of civ-ilized human beings. It is to the lack of such training that we owe the alarmingly frequent headlines to which I have just referred. In March 2008, *Time* magazine ran an article about British youth, describing them as 'unhappy, unloved and out of control'. Perhaps those three epithets are not unrelated to each other. Each of them has implications for parents.

The 'three Rs' of parenting teenagers

But let us return to Kate and John and their reluctance to face the issues surrounding Daisy, their errant teenager. For them and other parents, indeed even those whose daughters may be the Queen's Guide and Grade 8 clarinet player flaunted in a Christmas letter, this book invites some reflection under three headings.

Review

Even where children have been raised under good guiding principles, a parent may find it helpful to review how effective those strategies have been. As you reach this last phase of child-rearing, which will probably be the last opportunity for sustained uninvited input, should some adjustments be made?

> A wicked man puts up a bold front,
>   but an upright man gives thought to his ways.
> (Proverbs 21:29)

In my earlier book on parenting, *Aren't They Lovely When They're Asleep?*, I enumerated nine of the more common pitfalls in parenting. Proverbs is big on pitfalls: know what they are and avoid them, or at least avoid falling into them again and again. So, without apology, here are those nine, in brief, again – and with our adolescent in mind, let us ask ourselves some questions regarding those pitfalls.

- Allowing anything: Have I abandoned all attempts at setting boundaries? Do I fear confrontation? Who is in charge in our house?
- Bribery: Have I resorted to negotiation to get the behaviour I want? Is behaviour set firmly in a moral

framework? Are my children discovering the joy of doing the right thing for its own sake? Am I more concerned about the outward behaviour than the inward heart? Are my children only motivated by material considerations?

- Child-centred: Is our house revolving around this child and her needs? Does she think she is the centre of the universe? Does she know how to be, and not be the centre of attention?

- Distant: Have I thought of parenting as merely providing? Do I avoid personal involvement with my child? Am I more concerned for her achievements than for her? When was the last time I had a real conversation with him?

- Explosive: Do I boil over with anger and shout to make my point? Is it decibel level that moderates my children's behaviour?

- Fault-finding: Am I always nit-picking? Do I find myself continually comparing my child with other people's children? When did I last say something personally encouraging?

- Guilt: Am I trying to compensate for my own parental mistakes by buying them stuff? Do I ever say sorry to my children when I have behaved unworthily? Do my children know how to make me feel bad and manipulate me?

- 'Hedging' – by which I mean attempting to control your children by narrowing the environment in which they function: Are my children learning to use independence well? Do they have freedom to fail?

- Inconsistent: Am I only concerned about my children's behaviour when other parents are watching? Do I make threats or promises and not deliver? Do my

children know that I mean what I say? Do I give
a clear and consistent message about what is
important?

Even a short reflection on the above may reveal where you
have been letting things slip. The book of Proverbs is very real
about the making of mistakes. Again and again, it is saying to
us that the wise person is not the one who never makes mistakes. (Does such a person exist, in truth?) The wise person is
the one who makes a mistake and is not too proud to admit it
and learn from it so as not to repeat it. This is tremendously
encouraging and optimistic! It is not too late to learn and to
change.

> When pride comes, then comes disgrace,
>   but with humility comes wisdom.
> (Proverbs 11:2)

> Whoever loves discipline loves knowledge,
>   but he who hates correction is stupid.
> (Proverbs 12:1)

Regrets

The parenting road is strewn with regrets. Is there a parent
alive who would say that he or she got it perfectly right?
When you read the above list of questions, did you blush? I
will freely admit to you that I have many regrets about what
I did or what I left undone with my children. I wish I'd known
then what I know now.

  If you have embraced a deterministic worldview, then you
have no place to go at this point. It's all up, the die is cast and
you are to blame. Some people read Proverbs 22:6 determin-
istically. It says this:

Train a child in the way he should go,
   and when he is old he will not turn from it.

Many Christians read that and assume that if all the correct
components in the training are present and correct, the child
will emerge at the end of the parenting conveyor belt bright
and shiny and just as you would want her to be. Furthermore,
they look at a rebellious youngster at church and judge that
the parents must be at fault. Or, when viewing their own wild
child, they bitterly blame God for reneging on his promise.
But determinism is not the Bible. The book of Proverbs is
consistent in teaching that there is one, and only one, right
way. It is much more likely that a child will become a responsible adult if trained in the right path. But this is not a promise
or a guarantee; it is just saying that, all things being equal, this
is the way things tend to go.

   The book of Proverbs (as the whole of Scripture) is also
wonderfully balanced in its teaching on the sovereignty of
Almighty God alongside the responsibility and accountability
of humankind, his creation. Take, for example, Proverbs
16:1–6.

   [1]To man belong the plans of the heart,
      but from the LORD comes the reply of the tongue.

Verse 1 is telling us that a proper recognition of God's sovereignty over our future and our children's futures will
produce in us an appropriate humility. We have our plans and
hopes and dreams, but these may be overruled by his
purposes.

   [2]All a man's ways seem innocent to him,
      but motives are weighed by the LORD.

Verse 2 reminds us that we are always all too ready to deceive ourselves about how right we are or have been in our behaviour or attitudes. When it comes to reviewing our own parenting we tend to be very defensive about the choices we have made. It is important to remember that God is the final arbiter of what is right and wrong and he sees what goes on beneath the surface.

> ³Commit to the LORD whatever you do,
>   and your plans will succeed.

Verse 3 recommends that all planning be done in recognition of the fact that God can overturn it. We would be well advised continually to submit our entire life's action, including the raising of our children, to God.

> ⁴The LORD works out everything for his own ends –
>   even the wicked for a day of disaster.

Verse 4 is a further statement of God's control. God can use the very act of human (or teenage) rebellion and autonomy for his own purposes. We may not always understand those purposes in the short term. We may find them painful in our experience. But there is also comfort in knowing that evil will be punished.

> ⁵The LORD detests all the proud of heart.
>   Be sure of this: They will not go unpunished.

Verse 5 underlines the serious danger of pride. It is pride that makes children (and adults) unteachable. God holds your children accountable for their response to your training as surely as he holds you responsible for that careful training.

⁶Through love and faithfulness sin is atoned for;
   through the fear of the LORD a man avoids evil.

Verse 6 is good news for all of us guilty parents. There is something to be done with guilt. Sin cannot and should not be denied or minimized, but it can be made up for or covered over. Not by us! We could never do enough to make up for the offence we cause to the majestically holy God. The Old Testament sacrificial rituals pointed the way to the death of Jesus Christ, whose blood alone can reconcile us to God. Because of what Jesus did on the cross, believers can be and are forgiven. Their sin and guilt is covered over. It was the love and faithfulness of God that was the driving force of that death on the cross.

At a much lower level, the principle of love and faithfulness will encourage the failing parent. Certainly you will make errors as a parent time and again. But in parenting, a solid love for, and commitment to, your child will cover a multitude of sins. Your child will not be irreparably damaged by your mistakes as long as he or she is aware throughout of your unflinching love. What we need at all times, in order to keep a steady path, is a proper mindset, which puts God at the centre of things. That mindset in Proverbs is called 'the fear of the Lord'.

So, fellow parent, do not be overcome with regret. Understand and embrace God's sovereignty as well as his faithfulness and love, which means forgiveness for those like you and me who have messed up. And understand that both you and your teenager are work in progress. There is still work to be done. Don't give up hope – the Bible gives us every reason to hope.

Relate
Discipline problems in the teenage years nearly always boil

down to a failure in relationship. This is one of my favourite parenting sayings:

Rules without relationship lead to rebellion.

When you have a teenager, you are made very much aware that your authority is waning. If you go into your teenager's bedroom on a Monday morning and tell him it's time to get up and go to school, and he pulls the duvet over his head and grunts and turns over with the very clear message that he does not intend to rise at all, what do you do? You can pull the bedclothes off, but you can't pull him out of bed. He is 6 feet tall and weighs 11 stone. You can rant and rave at him as much as you like, but you cannot make him do what he has decided not to do. That is why I said earlier that you must hope and intend that your authority will become influence.

It is your influence which will persuade your child to do what he doesn't really want to do. And you will have no influence over him unless he trusts you. You will have no influence unless you have a warm relationship. Teenagers are acutely sensitive to the attitudes of adults towards them. All your good advice will go unheeded if your son is unconvinced that you really, genuinely like him.

It is harder to relate to a teenager than it is to a younger child. With a younger child you can tickle or tease; you can make her laugh, you can play with her toys, or join in her games. A small child will get up in the morning beaming and sunny and entirely forgetful of the fact that when she went to bed the previous evening, some necessary hard words were said. Not so, the teenager. The teenager remembers and broods.

A teenager is less accessible to you, the parent, for the following reasons.

- He has discovered the truth: you are not perfect as he once thought you were. You are well and truly off your pedestal.
- He has most of his social needs met by his peer group. He doesn't need your input when he has theirs.
- He is very busy with other agendas: his grades, his spots, his feelings for the girl over the road – agendas with which you might not necessarily sympathize.
- He has developed his own interests in music, reading materials and leisure activities, which don't necessarily coincide with yours.
- He is on the receiving end of many messages which are anti-parent.
- He is inclined not to like himself very much and fears that you share his opinion.
- He sometimes suspects that you only communicate to disapprove.

In summary, your teenager occupies a different world. And that is his perception as well as yours. Other friends, other technologies, other issues make his statement 'You don't know what it's like . . .' absolutely true. Even your concept of the role of the traditional family is one he may not recognize. After all, countless numbers of his classmates will be doing it differently. 'What's wrong with that?'

These realizations will not all happen at once, but will be gradual. They will be largely unspoken. Because of those barriers, you have to put in extra effort to keep the relationship warm and positive, to maintain trust and the sense of belonging together. How to do so is part of the subject of this book.

It is my prayer that readers of this book will be encouraged to think biblically about their teenagers and about themselves. Then they can go about the task of raising their children through this last transitional stage with hope and confidence in God and a genuine delight in those unique human beings with whom God has entrusted them.

For further thought or discussion

1. How would you try to encourage Kate and John to attend that meeting at their church about parenting?

2. Review your work as a parent to date. Which of the pitfalls are you most inclined to slide into?

3. What key truths of Scripture have most bearing on your work of parenting?

4. Why should you not be surprised at the least lovely aspects of your teenage son or daughter?

5. Spend some time admitting to yourself your regrets. Turn these into prayers of confession and contrition before God. What comfort can be drawn from 1 John 1:8–10?

6. Work on some plans to improve and enhance your relationship with your teenager. Are there some routines you need to adjust, or some interests you need to take up?

7. Make a list of things you really appreciate about your son/daughter. Think up some different ways to express that appreciation and support.

2. THE FAITH FAMILY AND THE FAITHLESS WORLD

Rachel sighed with relief as she and Tim and the children sat down in their usual pew at church. It was always a massive effort to get everybody breakfasted, booted and suited for morning service. She noted with satisfaction that the girls looked neat and trim in their new skirts. Sunday was the only day in the week when they didn't wear trousers and this had become something of an issue. At least Mark, their sixteen-year-old, had not demurred about wearing cord trousers instead of his usual jeans. His hair was rather long and untidy, however. Rachel observed with a touch of envy that the Watkins boys in the row in front all had short back and sides haircuts. As the minister announced the first hymn, Rachel glanced again along the pew at Mark, leaning forward to pick up his hymnbook. Heavens! What was that glinting in his ear? Could it be an earring?

Most young Christian couples are praying for their children before those children are born. Many will state unequivocally that their overriding concern for their children is that they should be believers in the Lord Jesus Christ. That is their number one ambition. With that end in mind, such parents will be careful and prayerful about their household arrangements. Their routines, their boundaries and their input will reflect that priority. If their routines, boundaries and input do not reflect that priority, then perhaps it is not the priority they say it is.

However, this ambition, deeply and sincerely held as it is, is not the same as other parental ambitions. You cannot get your child a place in heaven as you might get your child a place in a desired school. This latter might require a great many obstacles to be overcome, but people overcome them all the time, by fair means or foul. A place in heaven, however, is not a matter of overcoming obstacles. The one big obstacle to anyone getting a place in heaven, namely their sin, is impossible for us to overcome on our own account, let alone on anyone else's. Only God can overcome that barrier. And he has done it, through Christ's death on the cross. That death solves the sin problem for anyone who believes in Christ or receives Christ, which is the same thing.

> To all who received him, to those who believed in his name, he gave the right to become children of God – children born not of natural descent, nor of human decision or a husband's will, but born of God.
> (John 1:12–13)

Our children and God's children

God has children; he does not have grandchildren. If, in his sovereign kindness, it pleases God to save any of our children, that is entirely due to his grace. Much as we ache for our children to be converted to Christ, and pray fervently and frequently for that event to take place, we do not have God over a barrel on this. He owes us nothing. And no-one sneaks into heaven on the basis of his parents' faith.

Much Christian agonizing over the wayward behaviour of their teenage offspring is aggravated by forgetting or misunderstanding this point. We may look on our children as Christians because they say their prayers so sweetly, under our tutelage. Or because they love it at holiday Bible club or at Christian camp. Or because they know all their memory verses or are impeccably behaved at Sunday school. But we need to remember that it is one thing to be eager to please your parents or Sunday school teacher, and quite another to be eager to please God. A heart which wants to please God is something which God alone gives, by his Spirit. It is commendable when our children are well behaved, but it is not an evidence of saving faith.

Don't miss the point

So we should not be shocked at the worldly desires and behaviour of our offspring, which will become more evident as they grow up and enjoy more freedom. We can put a Christian sticker over the top and insist on certain outward conformity. This is Rachel's and Tim's approach – an approach which may impress our Christian peers at church, but it does not impress God. Neither does it make a scrap of difference to the heart condition of Rachel's and Tim's children, however good they look.

> Like a gold ring in a pig's snout
> is a beautiful woman who shows no discretion.
> (Proverbs 11:22)

But the worst thing about this approach is that it can lead a parent to miss the point entirely. It can lead a parent to be very wound up about a pierced ear, which may or may not be indicative of a spirit of rebellion towards God. But that same parent will not be concerned that her daughters, beautifully turned out as they are, are sitting demurely in church and spending the entire sermon thinking about flirting with boys, new handbags and the latest celebrity gossip. The preoccupation with externals can creep up unawares on those parents whose ultimate concern really is, or ought to be, new birth. However, such a preoccupation is at best a trivial distraction, at worst a harmful hypocrisy of Pharisaical proportions.

The advantages of a Christian upbringing

Is there then no spiritual advantage we can give our children? In one very important sense, no. There are no degrees in lostness, or deadness. And that is what our children are: lost and dead, until God effectually calls them, finds them, gives them life in Christ.

In another sense, however, the child born into a Christian family has immense advantages. All parents shape their children's thinking, the way they will look at the world. Neutrality is one of the great myths of the age. By what you and I do and say and do not do and say with our children, we are continually modelling patterns of thought and behaviour. It was always meant to be this way. It is part of what parenthood is about.

Some people pride themselves on their neutrality. 'Propaganda and brainwashing is what religious people do,' they would say with pride. 'We will not attempt to influence our children and we have told them so.' But even that statement is a philosophical position which could equally be described as influence or propaganda. That is why I say that there is no such thing as neutrality.

So the ethos of a household, whether it is atheistic, Christian, materialistic or sun-worshipping, is an influence, conscious and unconscious, on your child. The child from a Christian home will have the advantage of being exposed to, indeed taught, the gospel from the earliest age. And not just the gospel, but the whole idea that our very significance as human beings derives from the fact that we are made in God's image and inestimably precious to him. It is from the foundation of God's revelation of himself in Scripture that we derive and promote our understanding of goodness and truth. If your life is based on that foundation, your children will know right from wrong; their consciences will be instructed through your training. This thinking provides the pegs on which to hang the gospel when they hear it. Your children, through your teaching, will learn the way of salvation and understand why they need to take it.

Your children will have, on a daily basis, before their eyes, the example of someone who lives for Jesus Christ, if that is what you are doing.

Your children will meet, through your involvement in a sound Bible-teaching church, many other excellent role models at various ages and stages in life, who will show them what it is to be a Christian.

Your children will probably have the opportunity via the local church to enjoy, free of charge, wholesome activities designed for children and organized by trustworthy people in a safe environment.

These are just a few advantages which await that happy child who is born into a Christian home. They will promote his or her security and stability and self-worth. They will generally, at the very least, make your child into the kind of pupil every teacher will be grateful for and, in due course, the kind of citizen the government should be grateful for.

Added to this, your child will be preached to and your child will be prayed for. Since God chooses to save people through the 'foolishness of preaching' and frequently does so in answer to his people's prayers, your child is very well placed indeed. You have every reason to keep praying and trusting that those prayers will be answered at the time that God sees fit to answer them.

A godless and faithless world

Not only is no household neutral in matters concerning God, no culture or society is neutral concerning God. The Bible is clear that Christians live as pilgrims and strangers in a world in rebellion towards its Maker. The world at large declares, against the evidence of nature and the promptings of conscience, that it does not want to know God. Romans 1 tells the reader that therefore God let the human race have what it wanted: a godless world in which every kind of disgraceful perversion is evidence not only of the sinful human heart, but of God's judgment on that sin. So the Christian family is an oasis of faith in a faithless world. And the messages of that faithless world ring out very often in direct opposition to the presuppositions of the Christian home. These are the two paths presented in Proverbs, between which two paths the young person (and indeed every person) must take extreme care to choose.

> There is a way that seems right to a man,
>   but in the end it leads to death.
> (Proverbs 16:25)

The distinctives of a Christian home

Like the writers of Proverbs, Christian parents take some things for granted. They are not out to prove them; they are assumed. They can be grouped in three main categories.

1. Fear of God

For the writers of Proverbs, God's existence was a presupposition, the evidence for which was manifest in history and nature. In a similar vein, a Christian parent will marvel at the wonderfully made child in his arms and reflect:

> Ears that hear and eyes that see –
>   the LORD has made them both.
> (Proverbs 20:12)

This understanding of the way that God made the world, furnishing it as the perfect habitat for humankind, will profoundly influence the way parents organize their home life. Compare the following verses:

> By wisdom the LORD laid the earth's foundations,
>   by understanding he set the heavens in place;
> by his knowledge the deeps were divided,
>   and the clouds let drop the dew.
> (Proverbs 3:19–20)

with these words:

> By wisdom a house is built,
>   and through understanding it is established;
> through knowledge its rooms are filled
>   with rare and beautiful treasures.
> (Proverbs 24:3–4)

The Creator built wisely and so should we. The Christian should know that it is not the stuff you can buy from Mothercare which will provide the optimum context for raising a child. It is wisdom, something money cannot buy, which will furnish a home with real treasure. Wisdom, in the book of Proverbs, is an insight into the way the world works and the ability to make sound moral choices.

There is no real wisdom apart from a proper attitude to, and relationship with, God. This is described in many places in Proverbs as 'the fear of the Lord'.

> The fear of the LORD is the beginning of wisdom,
>   and knowledge of the Holy One is understanding.
> (Proverbs 9:10)

In his commentary on Proverbs, Tremper Longman III sheds light on the expression 'the fear of the Lord'. He writes: 'The verb "fear" has a semantic range that goes from "respect" or "awe" to "utter terror". What is indisputable is that to fear God is to stand in a subservient position to him. It means that you will acknowledge your dependence on him.'

If the expression 'fear of the Lord' is abhorrent to modern people, who would prefer, if they talk of God at all, to talk of loving him rather than fearing him, that is because our sinful, darkened minds have diminished God to something cosy and manageable. Wiser people know that fear comes first as we consider the very dangerous holiness of God. ''Twas grace that taught my heart to fear and grace my fears relieved,' wrote John Newton in his hymn 'Amazing Grace'. The fear of God was where it started for him.

This fear is helpful in keeping us in our place, putting the best of our skills and insights into a proper perspective.

> Do not be wise in your own eyes;
>   fear the LORD and shun evil.

> This will bring health to your body
>> and nourishment to your bones.
> (Proverbs 3:7–8)

This fear of the Lord is a crucial requisite for healthy living.

How will this attitude be demonstrated in the life of a Christian family? The answer is in a range of components which become part of the family routines. For example:

- family prayers;
- saying grace at meal times;
- involvement in a local church;
- Bible reading;
- a concern for goodness and truth;
- an emphasis on what cannot be measured or bought as opposed to what can, for example character as opposed to achievement.

All of these things are saying that God is important: he is the centre, not us; from him we have everything in our lives which is good; we must listen to him by giving attention to his word; we must let what he says direct our lives; we must submit our plans to him; we must be concerned about those things which concern him.

Repeatedly the writer of Proverbs stresses how precious is this fear of the Lord:

> Better a little with the fear of the LORD
>> than great wealth with turmoil.

> Better a meal of vegetables where there is love
>> than a fattened calf with hatred.
> (Proverbs 15:16–17)

2. Family structure

Christian parents accept that the family is God's idea. It is God's social service. It is his way of ensuring that children receive the provision, protection, direction, instruction and correction which they need. After all, they arrive in the world unable to provide for themselves, vulnerable, lost, ignorant and wayward. In order for provision, protection, direction, instruction and correction to take place, there is a built-in authority structure to the family. Although each member of the family is equally precious and worthy of respect because each of them is made in God's image, children are subject to their parents. Their parents are right to expect and train in obedience. This is not because the parents are bigger, stronger, older or cleverer, but just because they are parents. This is the way it is supposed to work. And it works for the children's benefit.

> Listen, my son, to your father's instruction
>   and do not forsake your mother's teaching.
> They will be a garland to grace your head
>   and a chain to adorn your neck.
> (Proverbs 1:8–9)

Parenting is not a consultation exercise, nor is the child's behaviour a matter for negotiation or bribery. There is an unquestioned order to family life, an order which the parents themselves recall from their own upbringing.

> Listen, my sons, to a father's instruction;
>   pay attention and gain understanding.
> I give you sound learning,
>   so do not forsake my teaching.
> When I was a boy in my father's house,
>   still tender, and an only child of my mother,

he taught me and said,
> 'Lay hold of my words with all your heart;
> keep my commands and you will live . . .'

(Proverbs 4:1–4)

Therefore Christian parents do not need to have an authority crisis. They do not need to ask themselves, 'Do I have the right to correct/instruct this child?' They will know that not only do they have the right, they have the responsibility. It is their time to step up to the plate. They will know that it is the act of a loving parent to correct, even when it seems hard work.

> He who spares the rod hates his son,
> but he who loves him is careful to discipline him.

(Proverbs 13:24)

In fact, Proverbs goes even further and suggests that a failure to discipline and instruct a child is the ultimate cruelty, a shameful attempt on his or her life.

> Discipline your son, for in that there is hope;
> do not be a willing party to his death.

(Proverbs 19:18)

Thus Christian family life will be distinguished (to some degree) by:

- parents who are confident in their authority;
- children who are expected to obey their parents;
- clear, consistent boundaries;
- loving correction and encouragement;
- promotion of virtue;

- unashamed propaganda: good boys/girls are happy boys/girls.

> My son, preserve sound judgment and discernment,
>   do not let them out of your sight;
> they will be life for you,
>   an ornament to grace your neck.
> Then you will go on your way in safety,
>   and your foot will not stumble.
> (Proverbs 3:21–23)

> My son, if your heart is wise,
>   then my heart will be glad;
> my inmost being will rejoice
>   when your lips speak what is right.
> (Proverbs 23:15–16)

3. Focus on the heart

Although outward behaviour is certainly a subject for control and moderation, it is the heart which is the focus of the Christian parent's concern. While it is tempting to be satisfied with an outward conformity to a set of rules, it is a short-term satisfaction. Unless your child has internalized your standards and embraced them, it will only be a matter of time before he or she shakes them off. Attitude is everything.

> A discerning man keeps wisdom in view,
>   but a fool's eyes wander to the end of the earth.

> A foolish son brings grief to his father
>   and bitterness to the one who bore him.
> (Proverbs 17:24–25)

Wisdom is a heart thing. It is by definition internal and it will determine choice of friends, choice of pursuits, ambition, priorities, lifestyle, and every kind of behaviour. So, although a parent of a young child can control most of those things, if the heart is not touched, if the child is not won over to desire what is good and true, the long-term outlook must be pessimistic. That is why the father in Proverbs 4 is not interested in a superficial response. Actions and speech will flow from a wise character.

> Above all else, guard your heart,
>   for it is the wellspring of life.
> (Proverbs 4:23)

In practice, a focus on the heart will mean:

- a lot of time invested in developing a warm relationship;
- a lot of talking and listening;
- an evaluation and sifting of the many messages the child receives;
- a focus on character rather than performance;
- a recognition that the child's greatest need is a new heart;
- instruction about God, his law and the gospel of Jesus Christ;
- a pursuit of a relationship with God, the heart of which is worship;
- an appeal to the conscience in all matters of discipline;
- an implicit and explicit acceptance that since we are made for God, we will never find ultimate happiness apart from him;

- encouragement (without coercion, which would be unbiblical and pointless) to trust Christ.

> The path of the righteous is like the first gleam of dawn,
>   shining ever brighter till the full light of day.
> But the way of the wicked is like deep darkness;
>   they do not know what makes them stumble.
> (Proverbs 4:18–19)

That, in brief, is a Christian philosophy of parenting. That is not to say that it is held consciously. Perhaps it is never precisely articulated or considered. But any Bible-reading believer will hold, however imperfectly formed, those kinds of ideas about what a parent should be doing and what a Christian home should be like.

That is not the same as saying that a Christian will consistently or perfectly execute the various actions enumerated above. It is more or less certain that he or she will not. We live in a fallen world; we belong to Christ's kingdom, but that kingdom is not fully realized here on earth. God accepts us and calls us his friends because we trust in Jesus Christ, who died for our sins. The Bible talks about us as not yet perfect, but working and being worked on towards a greater degree of goodness and holiness. In this regard we are very much work in progress. For all those reasons and more, we fall short and God knows that we do. Nonetheless, the Christian home is distinctive.

Secular child-rearing

Christians do not have the monopoly on loving and well-disciplined homes. It would be easy to look at a dysfunctional family and pick holes in its ideology or practice, but for our purposes we will take the best kind of non-Christian family and spot the difference.

1. Fear of other people

Many non-Christian parents are very careful about their parenting. They would say that their children are the most important and precious part of their lives. They may attend parenting courses. They are very careful to read and take seriously everything that is written on the subject of parenting in the Saturday and Sunday supplements. Many will be concerned not only to be good parents, but also to be seen to be so. A picnic becomes an educational project. A children's reading group turns into a competitive activity, for which children are groomed by their anxious and over-eager parents.

Such parents frequently feel paranoid and guilty. Alison Pearson's book *I Don't Know How She Does It* memorably begins with a scene where the heroine is doctoring shop-bought mince pies to make them look home-made, in order for her daughter to take them to the school Christmas sale. She fears the scorn of other parents who would mark her down as a second-rate mother if she were known to be buying mince pies from a shop.

These parents desperately want to get it right, but right is not centred anywhere. They are swamped with advice, but have no way of evaluating it, except by the following criteria:

- what their parents did (and they turned out all right!);
- what their friends think;
- whether it seems sensible – which is measured by how comfortable they feel about it.

Fear of man will prove to be a snare,
   but whoever trusts in the LORD is kept safe.
(Proverbs 29:25)

2. Friends first and foremost

Although instinctively these parents feel they ought to be in charge, successive government policies and pop psychological ideas have undermined their confidence in their own authority. 'Do I have the right?' is a serious question. 'What about self-expression? If I confront, will he be discouraged? If I correct, will I damage her self-esteem?'

So the secular parent has come up with a range of strategies for behaviour management. When faced with unacceptable behaviour, he is inclined to excuse, deny, bribe, divert, placate, consult or negotiate; he will do anything, in fact, except insist on obedience. It's a wearying and demanding process as every would-be instruction is phrased brightly as a 'would you like to. . .?' invitation. 'Would you like to do as you are told?' is not a question anticipating a positive response.

Even where the above is an exaggerated picture, it is certainly true that such parents are generally more keen to be their children's buddies than they are to be their tutors or guardians. Therein lies the problem. They are so concerned to avoid damaging self-esteem, and rather to praise, affirm and be liked, that they fear to set boundaries and offer them as mere suggestions so that a child has no trouble ignoring them. Then, when their children's behaviour has embarrassed them in front of their friends, or ruined their day, they are shocked, angry or just exhausted.

3. Focus on performance

Even when parents base their child-rearing on old-fashioned common sense and so avoid the scenario above, the secular mindset will out. Its idols are money, possessions, appearances (physical and social) and fame. The children of parents who worship at those shrines will learn to attach immense importance to performance, style, status, celebrity and material 'stuff'.

These parents will talk a lot about the importance of opportunities. They will seek out agencies which provide such opportunities. The driving force behind all this is their desire for their children to be happy.

It is not that secular parents do not have values. They do. They have values as opposed to virtue, which they would spurn as outmoded. They hope their children will grow up to be pleasant and kind and may commend such attitudes. But they will teach their children, if not in word, then by example, that material things will make them happy and that certain kinds of things will make them happier than others. They will tend to invest a lot of time and money in achievements, academic, sporting, musical. They want their children to impress in as many fields as possible and they care very much what other parents think.

When is a Christian family not a Christian family?
The answer to this question is: when it has imported some of those idols mentioned above.

We should never underestimate how difficult it is to resist the invasion of rampant, aggressive secularism. Some Christian parents give up altogether and are indistinguishable from other families except on a Sunday morning. Other parents, like Tim and Rachel at the start of this chapter, resist firmly but get sidetracked into a list of dos and don'ts. It is sad to reflect that it is quite possible for a Christian family to be as driven by the fear of other people as any secular family. It is just that they have shifted the audience they need to impress to the membership of their local church.

In our concern to raise polite and well-behaved children, we might be just as guilty as our secular neighbours in thinking that externals are all that matter. When all our investment in our children has had that outward focus, we should not be surprised if at some point we are disappointed that our children deem the Christian faith to be unnecessary, whether their rebellion is headline grabbing or quiet and respectable.

A Christian family is not a perfect family and it should not pretend to be. We are raising sinners, like ourselves. Honesty is much the best policy in this, as in every area of life. Be under no illusions; harbour no pretensions.

The witness of a Christian family

Imperfect as Christians are, where kingdom priorities are unashamedly displayed, a Christian family will be easily identified by those who come into contact with it. Against the background of rampant relativism and materialism, robust biblical faith will be evident in family life in many of the ways I have described in this chapter.

Whether or not the children are yet born again, there is much to commend Christian family life, based on that robust faith. It is centred, ordered, loving and life affirming. Provided hypocrisy is avoided, there will be people in your street who observe you setting off for church and are frankly amazed that you can get your children out of bed at that time on a Sunday morning. Your family unity and togetherness, your stability and happiness, your ability to say 'no' and be obeyed, your generosity and unmaterialistic attitude may generate a cynical sneer, but will also attract a reluctant admiration, even envy. There are many other families who would like a slice of your family life, even while they despise your beliefs. This is no bad starting point for witness.

The point at which a person says, 'I don't think Christianity is true, but I wish it was, so that I could have a family like that,' may be the point at which that person begins to be receptive to the gospel.

For further thought or discussion

1. What are your greatest hopes for your child?

2. Why are there no guarantees that your offspring will be Christian?

3. What are the distinctives of your family life? Consider attitudes to money, goals, priorities and routines.

4. What are the important truths which underpin Christian family life? How do these help a parent to set priorities and manage behaviour?

5. When are you tempted to fall into Rachel's and Tim's mistake of focusing on externals?

6. How will you assess what is going on in your child's heart?

7. Think of some ways in which you can commend and encourage heart attitudes and character, rather than performance and appearance.

3. FOOLS, MOCKERS AND SIMPLETONS

It was New Year's Eve and sixteen-year-old Sonali was deeply unhappy. She locked herself in the bathroom and scowled at her spots in the mirror. Was it because she was so dreadfully ugly that no-one had invited her to a party? Everyone else was going to a party. Everyone else had friends; she had none, at least not real ones.

Her mobile rang. It was Mayuri.

'Soni, are you coming to Anna's party?'

'Oh no, I don't think so! I won't know anyone.'

'The rest of us are going. Come on, it'll be a laugh.'

'No, I'll just feel stupid. I don't know any of Anna's crowd. And I've got nothing to wear. And I've got this enormous spot on my chin . . .'

After the call, Sonali's mood was even blacker. 'There,' she said to herself, 'no-one wants me at a party. I'm hideous!'

The school history trip to Germany included a visit to a former concentration camp where visitors could actually walk inside one of the gas chambers. Miss Dobson had prepared her class carefully for this theatre of extreme human evil and misery. She was therefore shocked, embarrassed and furious at the sight of privileged fifteen-year-old public schoolboys (her own pupils) posing for photos with one another, miming suffocation with their hands round their throats and their faces contorted, and then giggling uncontrollably.

In August 2007, Garry Newlove, forty-seven-year-old father of three, heard a disturbance outside his home. He realized it was a group of youths vandalizing cars in the street, as they or others like them had done before. He went out to remonstrate and protect his property. The youths turned on him and beat him down. He later died in hospital with the bloody imprint of a trainer on his forehead.

The scenarios described above are genuine. They demonstrate the potential of teenagers for folly, whether that folly is naïve and ridiculous, in extremely bad taste, or downright murderous.

Do not be alarmed or outraged at the chapter heading, which is drawn from Proverbs 1:22. There are many pleasures in parenting and the experience of raising teenagers has many joys, which I shall outline in chapter 8 of this book. I am not denying that teenagers can be as charming as they can be infuriating. Many teenagers of my acquaintance are cheerful, helpful, diligent and polite. But the Bible never flatters or affirms in its description of the baseline of human nature without God's intervening grace. It is never a question of saying, 'They're quite nice really and all you have to do is bring the best out of them.' See, for one example of many, Titus 3:3. The Bible has a pretty negative view of humankind. In our natural state, however bright and shiny we appear, however lovable we seem to our parents, we are foolish.

In this chapter we shall attempt to answer the question, 'What are we dealing with here?' How shall we describe a teenager?

The word 'teenager' never features in the pages of the Bible. However, there is a rare glimpse of the young Jesus of Nazareth at the very onset of adolescence. Jesus was twelve years old when he attended the Passover feast in Jerusalem, became separated from his parents and was discovered in the temple, astounding the experts with his insights into Scripture. The sinless Son of God was not moody or stroppy, but he still had some growing to do. He went back to Nazareth with his parents and was an obedient son. There in Nazareth, we are told, 'Jesus grew in wisdom and stature, and in favour with God and men' (Luke 2:52).

If, during his teenage years, the blameless Son of God was still developing intellectually, physically, spiritually and socially, how much more is the average teenager? The teenager is an unfinished article. This is an important point to remember and should prevent us from being unreasonably harsh or discouraged with him/her or with ourselves as parents. Theatre critics do not review a play in rehearsal, when the production is incomplete and the actors are still reading from the script. The teenage years are a time for work on the production and direction of a unique member of the human race. Defer judgment.

Theatre critics do not review a play in rehearsal, when the production is incomplete and the actors are still reading from the script.

Defer judgment not just on 'bad teenagers', but on 'good teenagers' too. Even when your teenage son or daughter is developing in a more than satisfactory way, even when your heart's desire is realized and he or she has professed conversion, it is not 'game over'. Jesus looked for disciples, not converts. There is still work to be done.

Seven vulnerable areas for teenagers

At this time of growing there are particular areas of vulnerability which are worthy of a parent's attention. Since substantial sections of the book of Proverbs are words from parents to youthful offspring, it is helpful to survey the subjects most commonly addressed in those sections. Proverbs 5 – 7 and Proverbs 22:17 – 24:22 contain some very specific parental advice. It would seem that at the time when apron strings are loosed and the fledgling adult takes his or her first steps towards independence, danger points exist. There are places where he or she could come a cropper. These roughly shake down into seven vulnerable areas. So the directing parent is wise to focus attention and training on those areas. To do so is not to be negative, but to be realistic. Some of these seven areas may be negotiated with ease by the teenager in your house, but there will be others which will expose the fact that he or she is very much only half-finished.

1. Reckless commitments

My son, if you have put up security for your neighbour,
    if you have struck hands in pledge for another,
if you have been trapped by what you said,
    ensnared by the words of your mouth,
then do this, my son, to free yourself,

since you have fallen into your neighbour's hands:
Go and humble yourself;
   press your plea with your neighbour!
(Proverbs 6:1–3)

This is an example of teenage naïvety: a young man who is persuaded to stand as guarantor for someone else's debt. Perhaps he needed little persuasion: eager for friendship and acceptance, he has volunteered to take that role. It makes him look big. It makes him look like one of the gang. The situation described in Proverbs 6 may sound archaic, but the danger is very modern and real. Teenagers are tribal and as they feel they are outgrowing their families, they are often looking for a substitute or additional one. They can be inclined to be too trusting of newly made friends and this can lead them into a trap. They can find themselves recklessly committing themselves, their money or their time to ill-advised projects or liaisons. A modern example of this vulnerability can be seen in the popularity and potential dangers of internet chatrooms. Of course, communicating with people via the internet can be innocent and it could be argued that such activity meets a social need. But young people need guidelines and boundaries in this area, as in others.

I am not suggesting that you start logging on to Facebook after your children have gone to bed in order to check out their associates, nor that you borrow their mobiles and scan the address book. The father in Proverbs is not banning all associations with neighbours, nor is he listening in to his son's conversations. He is seeking to equip his son with the skills to cope with, or even to extricate himself from, the messes he will undoubtedly get into through becoming inappropriately involved with people he barely knows.

2. Laziness

> Go to the ant, you sluggard;
>   consider its ways and be wise!
> It has no commander,
>   no overseer or ruler,
> yet it stores its provisions in summer
>   and gathers its food at harvest.
>
> How long will you lie there, you sluggard?
>   When will you get up from your sleep?
> A little sleep, a little slumber,
>   a little folding of the hands to rest –
> and poverty will come on you like a bandit
>   and scarcity like an armed man.
> (Proverbs 6:6–11)

Many parents of teenagers will recognize this one. Organizing your time is a life skill and teenagers are frequently slow or reluctant to learn it. They live for the moment – and at the moment, the bed appears a much pleasanter and more crucial option than GCSE coursework, which will keep until later. Or, if not the bed, then yet another episode of *Friends* or *Scrubs*, so that the evening has all but gone before she begins to stress about her essay that must be handed in tomorrow!

Every August the British public is told that exams are getting easier. But even so, a teenager's parent is well aware that good grades are not given away willy-nilly to the student who, during the study leave of May and June, has spent his mornings in bed, afternoons watching TV and evenings out with friends. It is a worrying time during which a parent may be ridiculously comforted by the sight of a revision timetable. But a revision timetable is only lesson one in time management; lesson two is abiding by it.

3. Unhelpful role models

A scoundrel and villain,
   who goes about with a corrupt mouth,
   who winks with his eye,
   signals with his feet
   and motions with his fingers,
   who plots evil with deceit in his heart –
   he always stirs up dissension.
Therefore disaster will overtake him in an instant;
   he will suddenly be destroyed – without remedy.

There are six things the LORD hates,
   seven that are detestable to him:
      haughty eyes,
      a lying tongue,
      hands that shed innocent blood,
      a heart that devises wicked schemes,
      feet that are quick to rush into evil,
      a false witness who pours out lies
      and a man who stirs up dissension among brothers.
(Proverbs 6:12–19)

We are presented here with these portraits of a character: two parallel portraits of the same very unattractive and dangerous individual. These are graphic descriptions focusing a good deal on body language. First of all, the reader is given the observer's guide to a villain; secondly, the reader has the benefit of the Lord's view of this kind of person. God, of course, has the advantage of knowing precisely what is going on. To an impressionable young person, however, these guys look cool; that is why we need God's view and opinion. He knows what they are about and he hates them. But teenagers can be taken in.

If you have taught in secondary school or worked in young people's groups, you will recognize the devious character described here. He is a cool dude with a secret language. He can get others to do what he wants by a wink or a snap of his fingers. Others in the group or class are well aware of this language; they are looking for his approval all the time. This character can engineer mayhem but maintain a look of innocence. He is smart and funny; he can exercise charm when he wants to; and he is immensely powerful amongst his circle of admiring peers. But he is dangerous and unwholesome.

Teenagers are looking for role models as they grow towards independence. At this point in their lives they are deciding who they will be. Sometimes you can catch them doing it in front of a mirror, striking poses, pouting or leering. They are trying on identities and evaluating the effect of those identities on the people around them. They are unashamed copycats in this quest, because they need approval, not just from their peers in general, but from particular, dominant members of their peer group. These dominant members, who are perceived as having style and charisma, are the people they will seek to emulate. As such they will have a massive effect in shaping the developing character of the young teenager. Goals and priorities will be imitated, even when those goals and priorities are completely counter to anything recommended or embraced thus far in life.

Parents of children who go quite wild very often mention the influence of a particular person. One described how all the problems seemed to start when their thirteen-year-old daughter went to stay with her grandparents and met an extremely streetwise girl, with whom she continued to correspond. The letters from this girl to their daughter, letters which were discovered and read by the parents much later, revealed the secret life of their daughter, about which they knew nothing at the time, but which totally explained her bizarre and wayward behaviour.

Beyond the unhelpful role models of your teenager's personal acquaintance are the ones presented by the media. Take a walk into town and browse the magazines aimed at thirteen-year-olds displayed on the shelves of W. H. Smith. You will find within those publications extensive articles (well, pictures, mainly) on the antics of the most unwholesome array of 'celebrities' whose sole aim in life is to party and flirt. Many teenage girls drink this stuff in and shape their aspirations accordingly.

4. Sex

> At the window of my house
> I looked out through the lattice.
> I saw among the simple,
> I noticed among the young men,
> a youth who lacked judgment.
> He was going down the street near her corner,
> walking along in the direction of her house
> at twilight, as the day was fading,
> as the dark of night set in.
>
> Then out came a woman to meet him,
> dressed like a prostitute and with crafty intent . . .
> With persuasive words she led him astray;
> she seduced him with her smooth talk.
> (Proverbs 7:6–10, 21)

Chapter 5, much of chapter 6 and all of chapter 7 of Proverbs are advice on the subject of sex. Now sex is God's invention and a jolly good thing, but the emerging sex drive of teenagers makes them very vulnerable. The sheer quantity of teaching in the book of Proverbs devoted to this subject demonstrates both the strength of the temptation and the dangerous consequences that result from folly in this area. The Bible is well aware that sex (or perhaps what young girls would call 'romance') is what occupies the thought life of young people much of the time. Why pretend otherwise? And the Bible is not afraid to name things. This is no embarrassed 'birds and bees' talk.

More than ever in the twenty-first century we are being made aware of the sexual activity of teenagers. Because, over the last five decades, ancient boundaries (see Proverbs 22:28) have been quite cheerfully and deliberately removed, our children are more vulnerable than ever. Sexually transmitted diseases are at epidemic proportions amongst teenagers, many of whom mistakenly think that a condom is the answer to everything. Teenage pregnancy continues to rise despite expensive government programmes, increased attention to sex education in schools and more information available than ever before. The results of a 2003 study by the Institute for Public Policy Research indicated that 40% of British girls and 35% of British boys had sexual intercourse before they were sixteen years old.

Christians might be rightly disgusted and appalled at the kind of sex education programmes offered by most schools. The fact is that sex education occurs best in a home context. Saying nothing is foolish; leaving it to school is dangerous. Proverbs gives us the lead to instruct and discuss these matters openly, parent to child.

5. Money and style

When you sit to dine with a ruler,
   note well what is before you,

and put a knife to your throat
   if you are given to gluttony.
Do not crave his delicacies,
   for that food is deceptive.

Do not wear yourself out to get rich;
   have the wisdom to show restraint.
Cast but a glance at riches, and they are gone,
   for they will surely sprout wings
   and fly off to the sky like an eagle.
(Proverbs 23:1–5)

In their quest for identity, teenagers are impressed by the style that accompanies wealth. As they surf the internet and discover facts about their favourite celebrities, as they watch advertisements which blatantly sell not a mere product, but the identity which goes with it, they are taken in. They really think that they must have this or that make of shoe or phone or handbag. They admire people who drive a certain kind of car, or wear a certain kind of clothes, or enjoy certain kinds of expensive or high-status leisure activities. These are the delicacies they crave for themselves, delicacies which are deceptive.

Although many proverbs advocate hard work and are quite clear that hard work brings material as well as other rewards, that is not the whole story.

Riches must be kept in a proper perspective. Wearing yourself out to get or stay rich, being obsessed by keeping up a certain style or keeping in with certain affluent friends is an unhealthy and unrealistic way of living which can lead a person to forget God.

Give me neither poverty nor riches,
   but give me only my daily bread.

Otherwise, I may have too much and disown you
    and say, 'Who is the LORD?'
(Proverbs 30:8–9)

6. Alcohol (and other addictive substances)

Who has woe? Who has sorrow?
    Who has strife? Who has complaints?
    Who has needless bruises? Who has bloodshot eyes?
Those who linger over wine,
    who go to sample bowls of mixed wine.
Do not gaze at wine when it is red,
    when it sparkles in the cup,
    when it goes down smoothly!
In the end it bites like a snake
    and poisons like a viper.
(Proverbs 23:29–32)

There are, in the present generation of young people, many
thousands whose idea of a good night out is to get completely
legless. This hapless ambition is embraced by many well
beyond their teenage years. This is not a new problem and the
lack of self-control with drink is known in every generation.
However, increased licensing hours, cheap, easily available
liquor and increased spending power have caused an upsurge
in binge drinking habits among those who are still below the
legal age for buying alcohol.

Teenagers are vulnerable because they want to do something which they see as adult, but they lack the maturity to
know when to stop. This danger is compounded by the
current youth ethos which celebrates drunkenness, finding it
amusing and impressive. In addition to this, many of the
people they admire in the world of popular music, fashion

and film are famous for being 'bad boys and girls' with regular excesses of drink and drugs.

Drugs present a similar temptation and danger. So-called 'recreational' drugs may be available in many of the places where young people gather. In an effort to look big and cool, teenagers are drawn into experimentation, frequently with far-reaching and disastrous consequences. Cannabis is now known to be the cause of mental health problems in many young people. Both drink and drugs, even in small doses, have been proved to rob young people of the ability to think logically and sequentially. The 2003 study quoted earlier by the Institute for Public Policy Research on the habits of fifteen-year-olds found that 27% of British teenagers had been drunk twenty times or more; 35% had used cannabis in the previous twelve months.

> Your eyes will see strange sights
>   and your mind imagine confusing things.
> (Proverbs 23:33)

7. Attitude to parents

> Listen to your father, who gave you life,
>   and do not despise your mother when she is old.
> Buy the truth and do not sell it;
>   get wisdom, discipline and understanding.
> (Proverbs 23:22–23)

> My son, keep your father's commands
>   and do not forsake your mother's teaching.
> Bind them upon your heart for ever;
>   fasten them around your neck.
> When you walk, they will guide you;

when you sleep, they will watch over you;
   when you awake, they will speak to you.
For these commands are a lamp,
   this teaching is a light,
and the corrections of discipline
   are the way to life.
(Proverbs 6:20–23)

This kind of plea is such a repeated refrain in Proverbs that the reader realizes there is a problem. Here is a young person who thinks he knows best, wants to do things his own way, wants to throw off the shackles of his parents' rules and regulations. But here too is a person who is very liable to mess up in all manner of ways. In other words, here is a teenager.

Most teenagers would rarely allow themselves to be seen out walking with their mother or father; such behaviour would lay them open to ridicule and make them look like babies. How much more difficult is it, then, for a teenager to accept that his parents might actually be wiser than they look, and that following their advice would be the best, safest, happiest option. Even if the teenager knows and respects his parents' wisdom, he will be unlikely to admit it to his friends.

Vulnerability and opportunity

Those are the seven main areas of vulnerability that emerge in adolescence. They do so partly as a result of physical and physiological changes. Despite what many sex education programmes want to tell you, young children are not, and need not be, aware of their own bodies in the way that adolescents are. No changes have happened apart from losing their milk teeth and it is hard to believe they ever will. My son and his friend, aged nine, were talking about how they would like to appear in action adventure films. 'But', said my son's friend, 'I'll get a stuntman to do the kissing.'

Alongside the bodily changes of the teenage years, there is increased independence. A younger child has little spending power and his time and social life are largely organized by his parents. A young child's role models *are* his parents, but increased observation and understanding of them, alongside an exposure to the world, will cause him to see their imperfections. There are many interesting people and messages out there and the young teenager is as anxious to see what they have to offer as a crawling one-year-old is to climb the stairs. The trouble is that, just as the one-year-old can go up but only knows the kamikaze way down, so the teenager can recklessly adopt all kinds of personae and embark on all manner of adventures without a return ticket.

At the risk of being written off as a grumpy old woman, I could add that teenagers of the West in the twenty-first century are more vulnerable than ever in all of the above areas. They have more spending power than teenagers have ever had before, they are ruthlessly targeted and exploited by commercial enterprises, and they are encouraged to do grown-up things before they are grown up. Perhaps they are also less disposed than former generations to receive well the advice from a loving parent. Successive government policies have done all they can to undermine parental authority in the name of children's rights. Parents blame the government, governments blame the schools, and schools blame the parents. Meanwhile, a generation is growing up without direction or instruction, floating in a moral and spiritual vacuum. They could hardly be more vulnerable.

The parental response

A parent may observe these vulnerabilities and react in a variety of ways. One way would be to limit independence strictly and narrow awareness. Some parents think they can control this period of their child's life by issuing diktats or by sealing the borders. For example, a parent might decide to refuse any discretionary spending money, but how will that teenager learn how to spend wisely? Or parents might severely restrict contact with non-family members. But how can a young person learn social skills if he does not have the opportunity to practise interaction with all kinds of people? Organizing a timetable/schedule for all free time might appear to solve one problem, but it has created another: that teenager has not learned to take responsibility for managing his own time.

At the other extreme are the parents who cut loose the teenage boat with neither oar nor rudder. Find your own way! Enjoy! Experiment! Express!

But the teenager, despite what he or she may think, is not fully formed. There is still work for the parent to do. This, as Paul David Tripp says in his excellent book on raising teens, is the 'age of opportunity'.

If you can maintain a positive relationship with your twelve-, thirteen-, fourteen- or fifteen-year-old, if you can continue to have meaningful and warm communication, then you can have invaluable input. The way of the Bible is not to control nor to abdicate, but to equip.

Some examples

Take the issue of time management. The goal is that the young person learns to manage her own time successfully. In the early teenage years, a parent can set up some helpful boundaries and expectations. It might be that school assignments have to be finished before watching TV or playing on the computer. It might be setting a maximum time for any potentially addictive activity. It might be a strict bedtime rule. It might be asking her to make lists on Saturday of essential and optional activities. When the teenager proves herself responsible within those guidelines, ease up on the control. Tell her that you trust her to manage her responsibilities. It is better to start strict and plan to ease up. That way the parent can be the positive 'good guy'. If you start relaxed and then get anxious and feel obliged to chivvy and nag, you become the 'bad guy' and it is hard work. But the direction is explicitly from parent control to self-control, from restrictiveness to privilege. Like the parent in Proverbs, it is fitting to let the teenager know what the goal is. That way she herself can feel encouraged as she makes progress.

The subject of sex also needs an overt approach. The book of Proverbs has a father speaking clearly to his son about the dangers of inappropriate sexual activity. Boundaries are clear. But note that the father is not negative about sex itself. While recognizing unequivocally how strong the sexual urge is, he commends waiting for marriage, being perhaps embarrassingly explicit about the delights of sex in marriage.

> May your fountain be blessed,
>   and may you rejoice in the wife of your youth.
> A loving doe, a graceful deer –
>   may her breasts satisfy you always,
>   may you ever be captivated by her love.
> (Proverbs 5:18–19)

If such talk doesn't make the average teenager curl his toes and study the pattern on the tablecloth, I don't know what will! But the message is that sexual relations themselves are not bad. What is needed is the proper context, that is, heterosexual marriage. Sexual relations are proper to the home, not the outside world. But note the positive attitude to sensuality and sexuality when enjoyed in the context of marriage. The best defence against illicit sex is a strong offence: look forward to the pleasures of married life (for which you are not yet ready). For the present time the teenager needs to learn how to treat the opposite sex with respect and appropriately enjoy the company of a mixed group of friends. Guidelines can be set regarding opportunity for interaction in the context of group activity. With young teens, these activities will frequently be supervised in some way, but as they prove themselves responsible, trustworthy and considerate, the supervision recedes.

The second line of argument on the subject of sex is no less important, and it is found in chapters 7 and 8: 'Learn wisdom.'

The greatest need

The greatest need of the teenager is the acquisition of wisdom.

The greatest need of the teenager is the acquisition of wisdom. That is the big thrust of Proverbs 1 – 9. Get wisdom. Pursue it actively. That is the repeated refrain. Wisdom can be defined as an insight into the way the world works so that the young person can avoid the pitfalls of life. It includes the ability to think through the consequences of an action and thus is invaluable in withstanding temptation in all the vulnerable areas I have mentioned. It provides protection against the many unhelpful influences the young person will meet. We will examine strategies for the acquisition of wisdom later in the book.

But first, consider this question: 'How do you know whether your teenager is on the path of wisdom?' The book of Proverbs has this acid test: how does he take correction? In the book of Proverbs, the wise person is not the one who never makes a mistake. It is assumed, in fact, that we all make mistakes most of the time. The wise person is the one who learns from his mistake, while the foolish one doesn't.

> A fool spurns his father's discipline,
>> but whoever heeds correction shows prudence.
> (Proverbs 15:5)

> Whoever loves discipline loves knowledge,
>> but he who hates correction is stupid.
> (Proverbs 12:1)

When your teenager can hear and respond in an honest way to criticism, that teenager is set fair. The implication of the continual reiteration of the desperate need for wisdom is that young people can best be described as foolish. Such a description is not intended as an insult, but as a tender and loving assessment of the situation to be addressed. Some kind of folly is the default position.

What kind of fool?

There are three classes of fool described in Proverbs 1.

> How long will you simple ones love your simple ways?
>> How long will mockers delight in mockery
>> and fools hate knowledge?
> (Proverbs 1:22)

The simpleton

The class C fool is described as simple or naïve. Most teenagers, even the well-behaved ones, are in this class. We hope that is where they are, because these are the most reachable and teachable. They might be clumsy and geeky, they might slink around with a heavy bookbag and a hangdog expression, they make lists, they look worried because they *are* worried, they feel foolish most of the time and don't know where to put themselves, they scrutinize themselves relentlessly. They think that no-one has ears which stick out as much as theirs. They frequently lack moral direction and are therefore subject to being swayed by all kinds of fads and whims. In the story at the beginning of this chapter, Sonali's belief, against the evidence, that she was both friendless and ugly is an illustration of this kind of simplicity.

The mocker

The class B fool is the mocker. This is the one who is sullen and sarcastic, who sighs heavily, who knows everything and is pained at having to listen to you or answer your questions. The parent who insists on a particular standard of behaviour may be obeyed, but not without a sneer or sulk or remark about what a 'saddo' that parent is. The public schoolboys on the history trip, who could deride the memory of Holocaust victims and think themselves so witty in the face of advice and direction from their teacher, are classic instances of mockers.

The fool

The class A fool is described by the generic term for fool. His hatred of wisdom is deep seated and indicates a hardness of heart which alarms you. This teenager has closed her heart as well as her ears to correction and therefore has effectively closed the door to the best of advice, however gently it is offered.

These unhappy young people frequently present as unattractive and occasionally as threatening, especially if challenged.

> Better to meet a bear robbed of her cubs
>   than a fool in his folly.
> (Proverbs 17:12)

The teenagers who set about Garry Newlove in a spate of mindless and extreme violence proved themselves to be class A fools. One of them at least had a history of trouble and warnings, but he had failed to learn or benefit from the mistakes he had already made.

It will be quickly understood that if all teenagers were divided into these three classes on the basis of the 'taking correction and instruction' test, class C would shuffle and mutter and blush, but would take it, class B would reply with a rude retort and might or might not comply, while class A would not even listen, but would respond with angry, abusive rejection.

Surely no child from a good home would become what I have termed a class A fool! Perhaps it would be rare for a child from such a home to become involved in violence and lawlessness of the kind perpetrated by the teenage murderers of Garry Newlove. However, we all know that children from loving homes can reject those homes and those parents. We have seen how such rejection can break their parents' hearts. Rejection can take many different forms. There is physical rejection, where a child runs away. There is emotional rejection, where a child refuses to accept the parents' expressions of love. There is moral rejection, where the child repudiates the values which the family holds. And behind all that is a hatred of knowledge, a spurning of correction. This is a heavy subject which will bear further examination in chapter 7.

Whether we assess the teenager in our house as a fool, a mocker or a simpleton, the question that must be asked and answered is, 'How will this teenager become wise?'

For further thought or discussion

1. What do you learn about the teenage years from Luke 2:52?

2. Consider the seven vulnerable areas. Which of them pertain most to your teenage son or daughter at the present time?

3. What kind of people do you admire? What kind of people do your children admire? Where will they find good role models?

4. How do you as a parent tend to respond when you observe vulnerability in your children?

5. How does your child respond to correction? How would you classify the teenager in your home?

6. How does it happen that a child who has had a careful upbringing becomes a class A fool? In what ways can a parent intervene to prevent a child's decline?

7. Spend some time committing your child to God. Pray that God will grant wisdom.

4. ROUTES TO WISDOM

A letter from a teenager to a teacher after an incident of misbehaviour on the school minibus on the way back from a football fixture:

Dear Mr Barton,

I would like to apologize for my actions on the minibus yesterday. I understand that I should not have opened the can of lager that I had found in my bag as it was wholly unacceptable. I realize that I have put you in a terrible position regarding the matter. I have learnt from this mistake and promise it will never happen again.

Sorry again for the position I have put you in.

Yours sincerely,
Charles Welland

If every teenager is some kind of simpleton or fool and vulnerable in the areas I have described in the last chapter, what is the way forward? The teenager's greatest need is wisdom; but how will he or she get it?

Let us take as a case study the ridiculous, but true, story of Charles Welland, alluded to in the vignette above. We can imagine the comments in the staff room: 'That idiot Welland . . .' 'Found a can of lager in his bag, did he? Perhaps it walked into his bag by itself!'

Charles Welland (whose name I have changed) is certainly a work in progress. He is the kind of simpleton who thinks it would be hilarious fun to open and drink a can of lager when in his school uniform, following a school event, on a school minibus and in the presence of his teacher. There is more than a hint of mockery and bravado there. He would seem to be vulnerable concerning both drink and the need to impress his comrades. But he is not unreachable. Perhaps he curled his lip and hardened his heart at the inevitable reprimand. But he did not refuse to apologize. Although no doubt his written apology is forced and probably insincere, he did write it in his own hand. There is hope for Charles Welland and thousands like him. There is a route to wisdom.

Tremper Longman III, in the introduction to his commentary on the book of Proverbs, identifies four sources of wisdom and I am indebted to him for his analysis. A Christian parent would do well to consider all four in relation to the development of a particular teenager. These are not four alternative routes from which a parent can pick the most appealing. Each one has its part to play in the development of a wise young person, who, though still fallible, will be well equipped to handle whatever life will bring.

Route 1: Observation and interpretation

Four things on earth are small,
   yet they are extremely wise:
Ants are creatures of little strength,
   yet they store up their food in the summer;
conies are creatures of little power,
   yet they make their home in the crags;
locusts have no king,
   yet they advance together in ranks;
a lizard can be caught with the hand,
   yet it is found in kings' palaces.
(Proverbs 30:24–28)

At the window of my house
   I looked out through the lattice.
I saw among the simple,
   I noticed among the young men,
a youth who lacked judgment.
(Proverbs 7:6–7)

From a child's earliest days, he learns about the world through the observations of his parents. In his mother's arms, he is looking from his window to the street while she points out to him cars, lorries, postmen, cats, birds and hot-air balloons. That is how a child learns language; it is also how a child learns to organize thought. Similarly, while looking at a picture book on her father's lap, she is learning not only the names of things, but the relationship between things, their stories. Such learning is invaluable.

The days of being held in Mummy's arms, or cuddled on Daddy's lap, are in a young teenager's distant past, but the parent still has a role to play in collaborative observation and interpretation of the world. In a family where relationships are warm and healthy and communication is good, this kind of thing is going on constantly. As stories are enjoyed together via books, films or TV, observations are made out loud and discussion is encouraged.

There is plenty to observe. King Solomon was a great naturalist and loved to observe the ways of all kinds of creatures. He made use of such observations in teaching his son. Is there that kind of mileage in a wildlife television programme? Certainly there may be. Equally there is plenty to learn from a detached observation of human behaviour. For a number of years, two of our teenagers used to walk with me on a Friday evening to a local supermarket to buy the provisions for the coming week. Ostensibly they were there to carry the bags home, but we frequently enjoyed looking at the people we met or saw, making deductions from their shopping baskets, as no doubt these people did with ours. It was a game, but it was also an education.

Observation via popular media

Many families enjoy regular film nights, where they settle down together on their sofa to watch something they will all enjoy. Again this works at more than one level. There is a great feel-good factor in engaging in such an activity together, but there is also a natural opportunity deriving from all but the most banal films, to discuss issues, attitudes, behaviour, moral choices, emotions and priorities. Is the film true, not in the sense of historical accuracy, but does it say something that is true about the world or about human experience? If it portrays lies, what are those lies? In particular, what lies or truth is it presenting about those vulnerable areas mentioned in the previous chapter? What mores of social interaction with the opposite gender are presented? What constitutes being treated well by another human being? Boys and girls with their heads full of romance and/or sex need to have their expectations challenged and shaped.

I am not suggesting here that a parent turns a happy family occasion into a lecture on 'how things have gone downhill since my day', but rather I am proposing that to identify and articulate questions raised by a film, a book, a TV programme or a current event is excellent training and can enhance the enjoyment. You can do this with quite a light touch. It is an extension of what you did when you looked at that picture book and asked, 'What does the pig say?'

It is a route to wisdom.

One word of warning here: not all observation and interpretation is focused out there in the big world. We need to remind ourselves that we, the parents, may be the object of our teenage offspring's observation. In the current debate about teenagers and alcohol, it has become apparent that the source of many young people's supply of alcohol, and the modelling of the need for alcohol as an essential means to pleasure, is the home. Parents are sinners too. Many teenagers pick up from their parents that excess or carelessness in some areas is absolutely normal and OK. We have to ask ourselves: what unhelpful messages do our children pick up from us? Could our weaknesses or bad habits exacerbate their vulnerabilities?

Route 2: Instruction based on tradition

Listen, my sons, to a father's instruction;
    pay attention and gain understanding.
I give you sound learning,
    so do not forsake my teaching.
When I was a boy in my father's house,

still tender, and an only child of my mother,
he taught me and said,
  'Lay hold of my words with all your heart;
  keep my commands and you will live.'
(Proverbs 4:1–4)

Pay attention and listen to the sayings of the wise;
  apply your heart to what I teach,
for it is pleasing when you keep them in your heart
  and have all of them ready on your lips.
So that your trust may be in the LORD,
  I teach you today, even you.
(Proverbs 22:17–21)

Does it sound horrendously Victorian actually to instruct a teenager in this way? I imagine that most of us have in some way been influenced by the child-centred approach to teaching, which is big on starting where the child is and meeting his or her needs. I trained as a teacher in the heyday of child-centred education and gained much from its approach. Certainly we should be sensitive to the child and the stage of his learning; certainly his learning will be enhanced if he is interested and excited about what he is doing. When I have written about assessing the vulnerabilities of your particular teenager, I am in one sense being child-centred. A child-centred approach is essential if we are to get over the barrier that is naturally erected by teenagers against being made to look or feel like a child or an idiot. A teenager already feels like an idiot quite a lot of the time and doesn't need your reinforcement. And yet he knows that he is no longer a child and will resent being treated as such. This delicate paradox needs careful, individual and child-centred handling.

An agenda and a curriculum

Nevertheless, a child-centred approach is pernicious if it assumes that the child must always set the agenda and the curriculum. There is, or should be, in every area of education, a body of knowledge to be handed on. It is the height of arrogance to assume that we have nothing to learn from those who have been on the planet before us or longer than us. It is the kind of arrogance that appeals to teenagers, but it is not to be entertained for one second. Common sense tells us that it is extremely helpful to lean on the knowledge of others. The same teenager who sneers at your advice today will one day be telephoning you for the benefit of your experience in matters which are new to her. And that will be a mark of maturity. So don't be put off by teenage sneers: you do have something to pass on. You just need to find the right way to do it.

Talking about how and when you came by whatever wisdom you have is a good beginning. The singer and songwriter John Denver did it famously in a song when he recalled how as a child he went to his grandma's house and slept with a host of other kids and animals in a great big feather bed. But the song is not truly about a bed; it is about the importance of family and of simple pleasures which money cannot buy. Our handing on of wisdom goes down well in the context of stories.

Handing on of wisdom is also excellent when it comes in the form of the answer to questions. 'Why do you always do that?' might seem like a threatening question from the lips of a teenager and we are tempted to go on the defensive. But in fact such a question presents a wonderful (and biblical) opportunity to pass on some wisdom, provided that you can answer rationally, honestly and amicably. This is one of the ways in which the redeemed people of God were to pass on the truth about God and his intervention in their lives.

> In the future, when your son asks you, 'What is the meaning of
> the stipulations, decrees and laws the LORD our God has
> commanded you?' tell him: 'We were slaves of Pharaoh in Egypt,
> but the LORD brought us out of Egypt with a mighty hand . . .
> The LORD commanded us to obey all these decrees and to fear the
> LORD our God, so that we might always prosper and be kept alive,
> as is the case today.'
> (Deuteronomy 6:20–21, 24)

Handing on our own wisdom is a good exercise for us, the
parents. We may discover our own hypocrisies and it is certainly best to do so ahead of our children, so that we can
correct them. We may discover our own inconsistencies and
need to shape up. We may discover our own weakness and
failure and a need to repent. We will definitely discover our
own imperfections and would do well to be honest about
them. But none of those things necessarily negates the truth
of what we have to hand on, if that wisdom is biblical and
sound.

Formal instruction

The biggest and most important body of truth we have to
hand on is the truth about God, our Maker, and about Jesus
Christ, his Son, who came to rescue us. This kind of instruction may be delivered during a routine family prayer time.
But it is the kind of truth which should pop up all over the
place.

The Bible, and the book of Proverbs in particular, also has
a great deal to say about the practical aspects of handling life.
This too should feature in our formal instruction. Let your
young pre-adolescents understand about the vulnerable areas
before they face them. That way, they are better placed to
understand themselves and will not be taken completely by

surprise. They are forewarned of the dangers that await them.

Informal opportunity

Whatever is going on in a formal context, the informal is of equal value. A good time for the handing on of practical wisdom is when it comes up naturally in the context of the life and struggles we are *all* engaged in. A teenager will find it easier to receive when it is presented humbly, as one traveller passing on a tip to another. If evidence of its usefulness can also be presented, it is all the more convincing.

Choose your timing carefully. Good timing for the handing on of parental wisdom is not when the teenager is in the thick of a mess brought on by her own folly. It is very hard for either parent or child to be detached and calm at that point. Instruction is not a telling off, and to turn it into a telling off is to invite the teenager to shut the door on you. A lecture on the evils of alcohol is not best given when the errant teenager staggers through the door at 2am.

Of course there will be a time for a corrective word or a word of warning, but those kinds of words should not be confused with words of instruction and advice. Nor should instruction be turned into coercion, which would almost certainly fail anyway. Parental advice is given in the fervent hope that it will be accepted, but in the knowledge that it may not be.

> Listen to advice and accept instruction,
> and in the end you will be wise.
> (Proverbs 19:20)

It is important to understand that the teenager is himself responsible for what he does with the advice and instruction. Endless repetition is not helpful. And although the advice and instruction may be disregarded at the time, it is frequently the case that it is stored up for use at some later time.

Routes 1 and 2 are parent-directed. In routes 3 and 4, the parent is calling on other agencies.

Route 3: Learning from mistakes

There are some mistakes you never forget. The lesson you learn stays with you for a lifetime.

When I learned to drive, I was of course taught the importance of applying the handbrake when I parked the car. But one day, when I parked the car at my workplace, I omitted to do it. Later, I glanced out of my classroom window and saw a space where my car should have been and my car where a hedge should have been. After that I was always careful about the handbrake.

We all have countless examples of this kind from our own experiences. Lessons learned this way are painful, costly and embarrassing, and that is why they are not quickly forgotten.

The book of Proverbs is realistic about the propensity of human beings for making mistakes. As such it is immensely reassuring. It is not the end of the world to make a ghastly mistake, even though it may feel like it. It might well be the end of the world if you fail to learn from it. But if you will learn and adapt your behaviour accordingly, you have gained some wisdom. There is a net profit. That is what Proverbs tells us again and again.

> Whoever loves discipline loves knowledge,
>   but he who hates correction is stupid.
> (Proverbs 12:1)

So as a route to wisdom, this one can be efficacious when routes 1 and 2 have failed. A young person does not listen to all the advice about consistent, diligent attention to his studies. At the end of August his poor grades will sober him. You don't need to do the 'I told you so' speech. He will know.

Facing the consequences

This route to wisdom, however, is not merely commended to the desperate parent. It is a means of learning to be embraced by all. One can take the view that if a child won't listen, then let experience be the teacher. And that is undoubtedly true. There is a limit to what a parent can do. The best of advice and training from the most kindly and careful parents is sometimes rejected. It is then quite wise and correct to let the wayward teenager face up to the consequences of his or her own folly. This is harder to do than it sounds, because our instinct is always to protect our children. But the natural consequences of wrongdoing are our friend and there comes a point at which we should let them take their course. So resist the temptation to be a 'helicopter' parent, hovering over your offspring to avert disaster. It is both exhausting and counterproductive.

Facing the consequences means to some extent bearing the pain. A seventeen-year-old who totals the car should be made to pay the excess. It would be unwise for a parent to rush to make everything all right. The parent needs to point out gently that some bad things that happen are the result of choices the young person made. And while there is a place for forgiveness, there is equally a place for making the young person realize the consequences of her folly, which may be far reaching and call for an adjustment of expectations.

Opinions will vary on this point and it does depend a little on the individual child and his or her vulnerabilities, but I made a point of not being too diligent about checking that my teenage children had done their homework or coursework. As parents we had commended and modelled a serious attitude to assignments and promoted the principle (from our own experience) that work is to be completed before playtime commences. But beyond that I took the view that homework was their responsibility: the GCSE, when awarded, would go to them, not me. If occasionally our offspring were sloppy or lazy, then they had to meet their teacher's displeasure, and they did. They found out for themselves the pleasure of doing well for its own sake, not to get me off their backs. They found out for themselves that it wasn't much fun to get low grades when they knew they were capable of better. They found out such things by making mistakes. And I think they found them out more thoroughly than if I had lectured and insisted and checked and double-checked, even though they might have got more A grades that way.

But take a potentially more serious scenario. Your eighteen-year-old daughter has started dating a non-Christian. (The whole dating thing is difficult anyway, but this is an added complication.) She is well aware from your observations and instruction that this is contrary to your advice. She knows how sad you are about it. Short of locking her up, you cannot stop it. You can remind her of sensible boundaries, of course. But it is probably counter-productive to have a daily confrontation on the subject or to go into a sulk. You have to pray that this might turn out to be route 3 to wisdom. It is hard for you 'just to pray' (although there is nothing 'just' about it), because you want to be active. You want it stopped. You know that, if it is not, there could be very far-reaching consequences affecting the whole of your daughter's life. At this point you are called to walk by faith. No-one is saying that is easy. But it is what must be done.

Taking responsibility

Learning from mistakes is about taking responsibility. It involves a humbling admission that you and no-one else got it wrong. It involves the understanding that behaviour and attitudes can be changed, not always with ease, but it can be done. This is an important lesson for life, as is the lesson that there is such a thing as forgiveness and a new start. Isn't that, in effect, the gospel?

Christian parents of teenagers have to live out the gospel. We have to allow our children the freedom to fail. And when they do, we have to be there like the father in the story of the lost son, watching for the about-turn and running to meet them with open arms, ready to restore the relationship.

When to say 'no'

In the meantime, there is the painful process of watching them make mistakes. Does that mean a parent should never say 'no'?

'Can I go clubbing with Jodie on Friday?'

'I'll be spending the night at Dave's, OK?'

Of course there are times for saying 'no', for setting clear boundaries. It is not my purpose to make a list of what is and is not appropriate for teenagers to be allowed to do at certain ages. I reiterate what I said earlier about the wisdom of starting strict and easing up as you recognize that your child is learning to handle independence. But that strategy implies that gradually you have to allow opportunities for that independence to be exercised. Small steps in the right direction can be met with the encouragement and the permitted privilege of increased independence. Know your child. Choose your battles. That is my advice.

When I've been faced with a request for permission and it has been my strong instinct to refuse outright, I have found it helpful to use a delaying tactic:

'That's a tricky one! Can I come back to you?'

'Daddy and I will have to talk about that.'

It is amazing how often these problems sort themselves out. Situations and minds are changed; the child himself, sensing your concern, rethinks or rearranges. Apart from that, you have time genuinely to think and pray over it and you have avoided what looks like an instant out-of-hand negative.

If you make good use of route 1 (observation and interpretation) and route 2 (instruction based on tradition), then you need not fear route 3. On the contrary, it might be a perfect way of cementing those lessons you have endeavoured to teach, even if there are tears on the way.

If routes 1 and 2 have been neglected by you or rejected by your child, then route 3 will be a hard school. But you are running out of options in your desire for your foolish teenager to become wise. This one is out of your hands, but (it bears repeating), like Job, you can pray.

And pray you must. Although lessons learned from mistakes are powerful, they do not work by magic. If every teenage girl who allowed herself to be manipulated or encouraged into sexual relations, with a resultant pregnancy and abortion, learned from her mistake, then the abortion rate would drop dramatically. The evidence is that one mistake paves the way for another. It is similar with mistakes in the areas of drink and drugs. There are some who learn and change, but there are many who can't or won't. This is in itself further evidence of true folly.

> As a dog returns to his vomit,
>> so a fool repeats his folly.
>
> Do you see a man wise in his own eyes?
>> There is more hope for a fool than for him.
>
> (Proverbs 26:11–12)

Despite the gloomy prognosis for some, learning from mistakes is a well-trodden path to wisdom and parents should not be too precious or protective to embrace its use. But there remains one more route.

Route 4: The fear of the Lord

The other three routes, if followed, can deliver healthy, happy, civilized adults, but if those same individuals have not walked route 4, something fundamental will be missing. Proverbs tells the reader more than once that at the heart of wisdom is God himself.

> The fear of the LORD is the beginning of wisdom,
>   and knowledge of the Holy One is understanding.
> (Proverbs 9:10)

If wisdom is defined as the ability to handle life, avoiding its pitfalls, then ultimately such ability cannot be properly achieved without reference to the God who gave us life. He has to be the reference point because he is the centre of the universe and we are not. Without this perspective, a person cannot truly navigate life. There will be no meaning or purpose, no answer to the question 'Why *should* I?' The crucial ability to accept correction and advice is strengthened by the acknowledgment that everything is created and sustained by God. He is big; we are small. Even the ability to observe and experience comes from God himself. And as for our circumstances, we are wise if we acknowledge that those too are in his hands.

> Ears that hear and eyes that see –
>   the LORD has made them both.
> (Proverbs 20:12)

Many are the plans in a man's heart,
    but it is the LORD's purpose that prevails.
(Proverbs 19:21)

Such an understanding produces a healthy attitude to oneself
and the world with all its dangers and disappointments.

Beyond that, the fear of the Lord in Proverbs is relational.
When the father talks to his son so warmly about its importance, it is clear that this is driven by a passionate love for the
Lord. Knowing God not just as *the* centre, but as *your* centre
is what enables the father to make all the connections to the
way to handle life. It is not a matter of rules and regulations.

God, the giver of wisdom

The thing about this fear of the Lord is that you, the parent,
cannot impart it. It is God himself who gives it and he gives
it to those who seek it.

If you call out for insight
    and cry aloud for understanding,
and if you look for it as for silver
    and search for it as for hidden treasure,
then you will understand the fear of the LORD
    and find the knowledge of God.
For the LORD gives wisdom,
    and from his mouth come knowledge and understanding.
(Proverbs 2:3–6)

There is a kind of circular reasoning here. The young person
is encouraged to seek wisdom and find God. When she finds
God, she will find wisdom. It is like Jesus' words that to those
who have, more will be given (Luke 8:18). God is not in
the business of disappointing those who seek him. On the

contrary, he graciously gives to humble seekers more than they ever would have thought of requesting.

It would seem that the fear of the Lord is an Old Testament expression for what we know as Christian conversion. Certainly, the fear of the Lord produces in those who have it not only wisdom, but many of the blessings of salvation: healing (Proverbs 3:8), a refuge (14:26), life after death (14:27), victory over evil (19:23) and ultimate security (29:25).

What Christian parent would not desire this for a child more than anything? And if a child has this, he has in Christ all he needs for life, whatever else may happen.

> Better a little with fear of the LORD
> than great wealth with turmoil.
> (Proverbs 15:16)

Four things a parent can do

We know that we cannot save our children; we cannot instil in them the fear of the Lord. So what can we do?

Firstly, we can faithfully teach our children about God – not just Bible stories when they are little, but the whole doctrine of God. As one generation to another, we speak of his glorious acts, his mighty works, his power, his goodness, his holiness and his love. They cannot fear the Lord if they have never heard of him.

Secondly, we can commend the fear of the Lord. That is what the writers of Proverbs do over and over again. They compare it to the greatest treasure on earth, and so it is. One might set many worthy ambitions before a child: playing football for the first team, going to Cambridge, excelling in music, but this is better and more important, well worth giving up other smaller ambitions for. It is a source of fulfilment and enrichment beyond anything this earth can offer.

Thirdly, Christian parents can model the fear of the Lord. If being a Christian is so good, why do Mum and Dad make such heavy weather of it? Why does spending time with God seem low on the list of priorities? Why do they never speak of him except as a duty? 'Solid joys and lasting treasure, none but Zion's children know,' wrote John Newton in the eighteenth century. Perhaps twenty-first-century Christians need to display some more of that delight in their God and Saviour. It is salutary for parents to realize that everything they do has this by-product of modelling something to their watching offspring. One of our sons recalled his father bringing him a mug of tea every morning. He said long afterwards, 'I was well aware that Dad had been up for ages praying and reading the Bible. This made a huge, if subconscious, impression.'

Fourthly, we can pray for God to shine his light in the hearts of our children. If in his mysterious purposes he keeps us waiting in answering that prayer, we should not give up. Our children are more precious to him than to us. We can cry to him on their behalf and know that he hears.

If a parent is convinced that his daughter is converted, does that absolve him of any responsibility with regard to training in wisdom? Not at all! Proverbs commends all four routes. A converted thirteen-year-old has the best possible foundation for wisdom, but still needs training. She will still make mistakes and need to learn from them. She will still benefit from parental help in observing and interpreting the world. She will still find useful and necessary the wisdom you have to offer. The difference is that because the foundation of the fear of the Lord is there, she will be more receptive to the training. She will learn more readily from her mistakes.

The fact is, a parent can never be complacent. A soundly converted seventeen-year-old boy is still subject to temptations. He will still be hearing from every possible direction the insistent invitations of folly. We should not underestimate their power, especially when it comes to sex. Everybody is saying that it is natural and fine and dandy to sleep with your girlfriend. Only seriously weird or ugly people would not do it. Tragically, even in some Christian circles there has been widely accepted compromise on the Bible's very clear standards in this matter. There is still plenty of work for a parent to do.

And while you, the impatient parent, long for evidence of the fear of the Lord, and pray over the learning from mistakes, make the most of observation, interpretation and advice based on tradition.

For further thought or discussion

1. How does Charles Welland's letter to his teacher exemplify the folly of teenagers?

2. Why is there hope for Charles Welland?

3. Think of some contexts in which you can engage in route 1 (observation and interpretation) with your children. What must you be careful to avoid?

4. What advice and instruction have you to hand on to your children? Make a list of 'subjects' you think you should be covering at this present time.

5. How, when you all lead busy lives, will you make time for this kind of instruction, both formally and informally?

6. Recall a time when you learned from a mistake. Perhaps this is a story you could tell your children.

7. Is there an issue or situation where your advice has not been sufficient to impart wisdom? Is it time to allow your teenager freedom to fail?

8. Name your fears concerning route 3 (learning from mistakes) and your teenager. Pray over them.

9. Write down a number of reasons why the fear of the Lord is the best route to wisdom.

10. What are you doing to teach, commend and model the fear of the Lord?

5. MEET THE PARENTS

Ferris heard the ringtone from deep down in the bottom of his schoolbag. He rooted around, trying as he did so to keep up with his group of friends. They were straggling their way across the park, swigging cans of lager. Ferris looked at his mobile and sighed. Not that he was in the least surprised.

'Hello, Mum.' Ferris rolled his eyes at his friends, who had stopped to wait for him.

'Yeah, we're just walking down into town.'

'Yeah, I know, but like, I need some more paper for my file, for my coursework, you know . . .'

Ferris's friends started laughing and Ferris put a warning finger to his lips to hush them up. They immediately started miming cut-throats and being hanged. Ferris had some difficulty in keeping his voice steady on the phone.

'Yeah, there's like a few of us. Yeah, we all need paper . . .'

Ferris held the phone away from his ear while his mother poured forth a torrent of warnings.

> *When she paused for breath, Ferris continued, 'Yeah, but like I thought I might go to Ojay's house. There's a geography project we need to work on together.'*
>
> *Ferris's friends were by now bent double, stuffing their fists into their mouths to stop themselves laughing.*
>
> *'Yeah. I'll come back straight afterwards.'*
>
> *'Yeah, bye.'*
>
> *'Ferris! Man, how do you put up with it?' said Ojay. 'How many times a day does she do it?'*
>
> *'Not any more!' said Ferris with a wide grin. He switched off his mobile and stuffed it back in his bag. 'Is there any of that beer left?'*

The trouble with parenting, I always say, is that you can't get the staff. Talk to any sensible Christian parent and they will come up with the kind of principles I have been recommending in this book. No surprises there. It's the doing of it that's hard. So, if we know so much, why do we encounter difficulties? There are two main theological reasons:

1. Children are sinners
2. Parents are sinners

I have tried to address point 1 in earlier chapters, in the clear understanding that this a fallen world and perfection is for heaven. With that same presupposition in mind, let us turn our attention to point 2.

Parents who are also teachers sometimes observe that they find themselves perfectly capable of maintaining a calm, relaxed, even jolly disposition with the teenagers in their class, but completely lose it with their own offspring. Their wisdom and patience evaporate as they put their key in their own front door. Why is it that even people who are professional experts on teenage behaviour can be tense, irritable and grumpy with the adolescents who share their name and home?

Apart from being sinners, we find it impossible to have a professional detachment about our children. We care passionately about them. Caring parents (and most parents *do* care, I find) have a view about every aspect of their children's lives, from how they brush their teeth to what they watch on TV and what kind of life forms grow in their blazer pockets. It matters to them. And so it should.

We might think that we would do a better job if we were more detached, but we would be mistaken. God has decreed that the people who care most about their children should have the primary responsibility in shaping and directing their lives. Of course, there are practical reasons why we delegate some of that shaping and directing to others, for example in choosing a school, but we still carry the can and bear the pain. Our vested interest is in our children's interest.

Why is it such a sad thing to read of a childhood spent in a children's home? Because we know that although the house-parents may be wonderfully kind, they work shifts. They may be holders of tip-top qualifications in psychology and child-care, but at the end of the day they go back to their own homes to live their lives with the people who are most important to them. And at that point, the 'clients' they 'care' for as part of their daily work are legitimately forgotten. But parents *really* care for the welfare of their children, 24/7, as the saying goes. It is not exactly like our heavenly Father who neither slumbers nor sleeps, but it is after that pattern.

But non-detachment brings pain. Our heavenly Father knows all about that.

'A son honours his father, and a servant his master. If I am a father, where is the honour due to me? If I am a master, where is

the respect due to me?' says the LORD Almighty.
(Malachi 1:6)

It is axiomatic that as surely as we let God down, our children will let us down. Sooner or later, in one way or another, it will happen. Here we are, trying faithfully to teach our children, trying to do a good job at bringing them up in the training and instruction of the Lord. And we see evidence of a less than perfect response. We see dire disobedience. We see dangerous distractions. We are desperately disappointed and discouraged. There is nothing wrong with that. It is the price of love. But problems arise in our attempts to handle that disappointment and discouragement.

The fact is, we have invested so much in our offspring that we take it personally when we observe behaviour and attitudes which are less than worthy. We understand in general that teenagers can be touchy or rude, but when it is *our* teenager's touchiness or rudeness, we are personally wounded. Little do these gangling youths know what power they have to ruin our day!

So in this chapter we are going to look at ourselves, the parents. It is just possible that some of our attitudes and dispositions may be making raising a teenager harder than it need be. In some cases we may be fouling the very pitch on which we want to pass the ball of wisdom. We may, in effect, be scoring for the other team.

From my own observations, there are two emotions behind the furrowed brow or deep sighs of the average parent of a teenager: one is fear and the other is guilt.

From my own observations, there are two emotions behind the furrowed brow or deep sighs of the average parent of a teenager: one is fear and the other is guilt. One looks forward, the other backward. And each of these beauties has babies of her own, which generate further difficulties or misery.

Fear and her babies

Fear looks forward. If you really think about all the ways in which your children could go wrong or encounter trouble in the future, you might wish you had been sterile. Potentially, your children face unnumbered external dangers every day: strangers in raincoats, drunken drivers, playground bullies, orange squash with E numbers, serial killers, teachers with PMT, drug-pushers, unmuzzled Rottweilers, predators in internet chatrooms, falling hanging baskets . . . Stop! Our imaginations are extremely fertile once they get going on this theme.

And then there are the innumerable internal dangers: laziness, greed, craving for popularity, envy, self-pity, bad temper, pride, and so on and so on. What shall we do? There is a sense in which we have every reason to fear.

Fear's bad baby number 1: Anxiety

It is natural to be anxious, but it is not a good idea. It is bad for our health and contrary to the command of Scripture.

> Do not be anxious about anything, but in everything, by prayer and petition, with thanksgiving, present your requests to God.
> (Philippians 4:6)

Many Christians can trot that verse out with ease. It is less easy to obey – especially, I find, the thanksgiving bit. And yet the habit of thankfulness in prayer changes the whole way we look at a problem and genuinely dissolves anxiety. Thank God for your teenager; recall before God the many joys of his presence in your life; be grateful that this is still the day of grace and God has a massive cupboard of resources from which you and he can draw strength and wisdom for this day.

> Trust in the LORD with all your heart
>   and lean not on your own understanding;
> in all your ways acknowledge him,
>   and he will make your paths straight.
> (Proverbs 3:5–6)

Anxieties and fantasies

Our anxieties drag us down, but for the most part we are dwelling on things that haven't actually happened yet. A gloomy football supporter watching his team play a crucial end-of-season match may decide pessimistically that it is all over at 0-0 with twenty minutes still to play. He may be buttoning up his coat and preparing to leave the stadium, so convinced is he of defeat. But it isn't all over. That is why the teams are still on the pitch, playing the game. At that point either side could score and it might be the side he supports. So it is with our anxieties for our children. The game is still being played. Anything could happen, and not necessarily the bad thing.

Anxiety – a waste of energy

In our anxiety for our children, we spend time and emotional energy grieving for the disasters that might occur. What a waste that is! We exhaust ourselves imagining gloomy stories, picturing worst-case scenarios and working out what we would do next. But the game is not over yet. We don't actually know that the worst will happen. It hasn't so far. Why not use our energy in thanksgiving that it hasn't happened and prayer that it won't? If the worst does happen, God is big enough for that day. This is an opportunity to trust him and prove what he will do.

Fear's bad baby number 2: Control

We can alleviate our anxieties by going for control. Of course there is still a place for boundaries when your child is in her teens. You are utterly wise when you set times for turning up for meals or coming in at night. These are house rules which make it possible for the home to function efficiently and with due consideration for the other members. All that is good training. But you do yourself and your teenage child no favours when you are continually on his case.

In the story at the beginning of the chapter, Ferris's mother fears that he is up to no good. She fears that he is getting in with a bad crowd. She is not wrong, but her strategy is ineffective and counter-productive. She uses his mobile phone as a pager, to call him and check on his movements. Ferris, wearied and embarrassed by her inappropriate intervention, responds with lies. He learns to practise deceit. He learns to live a double life and to disregard with ease the wisdom his mother so desperately wants to pass on.

Control by schedule

Some parents control by running a very tight schedule. But the teenage years are the time for learning to take responsibility for time, money and friendships. If a controlling parent seeks to limit these savagely in the interest of alleviating his own anxiety, that parent is denying that teenager the opportunity to learn to manage well. Then, when that teenager finally makes a break for freedom, he will be ill-equipped to deal with it. What tends to happen to such teenagers, let off the leash, is that they go on the rampage, tasting all the forbidden fruits.

A better idea is to build into your child's upbringing increasing opportunity for him to take responsibility for himself. Alongside this there is training and instruction. Expectations can be made clear and demonstrated to be in the interest of health and happiness all round. But there is a point at which the young person has to be released to live his life and make his own choices, within the parameters you have set down at any given stage.

Control by sanctions

Some parents choose to control by sanctions. Although sanctions are appropriate when explicit and agreed boundaries have been crossed, a parent needs to remember that the long-term aim is *self*-discipline. The same applies to control by rewards. This kind of external negotiation to get the desired end-product is ultimately counter-productive. It does not tend to produce a young person who wants to do the right thing for its own sake. Extrinsic rewards and sanctions do not bring about intrinsic motivation. I knew a parent who bribed her daughter to volunteer as a leader at the church holiday Bible club. She promised her daughter money if she would participate. That parent was so desperate to see her daughter behaving like a Christian young person. This was a mother who was very anxious about the friendships her daughter was making outside the church. But although the daughter helped in the club, she had been denied the joy of choosing to give. She went through the motions; her heart was not touched. She took the money and ran.

Control by nagging

Other parents control by nagging. There are an intriguing number of references in Proverbs to the vexation of living alongside a nagging or quarrelsome wife (21:9; 21:19; 25:24;

27:15–16). In each case the word translated 'wife' could equally be translated 'woman'. So a teenager living with a nagging mother might concur:

> Better to live on a corner of the roof
>> than share a house with a quarrelsome woman.
>
> (Proverbs 21:9)

A nagging mother, or father, is very likely to drive a teenager to put a 'keep out' sign on his bedroom door. His bedroom or his friend's bedroom will become his 'corner of the roof'.

Control by manipulation

Lastly, there is control by emotional manipulation. Parents are capable of clever power games whereby they limit their children's independence by making them feel bad. So a father can make his son feel responsible for the father's happiness or reputation. He has to perform well in school or on the sports field, otherwise he will let his father down badly. Teachers tell of parents who come to a parent interview evening with high academic ambitions for their children. But those parents are blind to their child's actual abilities, which lie in a completely different direction.

Sometimes young people are pressurized, channelled and manipulated into making choices which push all the right buttons for their parents, but are a long way from what they themselves want. Further down the line for such children and their parents there is the anguish of failure and in addition a huge well of resentment. The 1980s film *Dead Poets Society* movingly portrayed such a family. In that story, a talented young man became so angry at his parents' failure to listen that he took his own life.

We need to remember that the aim of getting our children to make wise choices is not so that we feel better or look good. That is not the point. Our children are to do the right thing because it is the right thing and because that is the only way to a healthy life. More importantly, it is God's glory that matters, not ours. Beware of managing your anxiety by emotional manipulation. It leads to a very angry child.

Fear's bad baby number 3: Anger

Fear can often surface as anger. Have you ever witnessed the reunion of a mother with a child who has been lost in Sainsbury's? There may be tearful hugs, but there will also be a telling off. Teenagers do not get lost in Sainsbury's; they go absent without leave in other ways. And on their return they will often face an anger which is driven by fear.

This fear turned to anger can manifest itself over quite trivial incidents. You find, as the parent of a teenager, that there are things you do not like in the choices he or she makes. My husband still recalls the first time we allowed our eldest son, aged about thirteen, to choose the way the barber cut and styled his hair. Our son remembers it too because of the brouhaha that ensued. It was a critical moment in our recognition that our son was growing up and that he had his own opinions on matters beyond the application of hair gel.

This happens in every generation. If their bad taste matched the bad taste of *your* youth, perhaps you would have less to complain about. But each generation finds its own bad taste. 'People try to put us down just because we get around,' sang The Who in that anthem of angry youth, 'My Generation', way back in the mid-1960s. I loved it and I was a teenager at the time. But my parents had a different perspective. Although rows may be sparked over clothing, earrings or tattoos, the parents are angry less because their good taste is offended than because underneath it all they are afraid. There is an element of self-seeking pride in this fear. A parent is frequently afraid of what people will think.

But there is a deeper, darker fear. It is the fear over what this latest manifestation of teenage independence represents. Is it the beginning of a slippery slide into bad company, unhealthy lifestyle, or even addictions? Well, of course it might be. But equally it may be a teenager just being a teenager, trying on an attitude for size. Get out the ancient photograph album and peer at yourself when young. Note the telltale signs of rebellion in the hair, clothes and eyes. Was that weirdo already fully set on the delinquent road to ruin? I do not mean to make light of genuine parental concerns. I just mean to suggest a sense of perspective. Also, do remember that the disaster you fear hasn't happened yet.

Anger – rarely a solution

Anger, although it is an understandable response, is rarely a solution in parent–child confrontations, whether the offence is trivial or serious.

> It is to a man's honour to avoid strife,
>   but every fool is quick to quarrel.
> (Proverbs 20:3)

Discipline remains a parental responsibility. Breaches of discipline should not be ignored, but an angry response is counter-productive, especially with a teenager. You can frighten a young child into obedience, although I am not saying that is a good idea. Nevertheless, it can be done. But if you lose your rag with a teenager, you will just make her angry in return. You will invite her to stomp off and slam the door. And although you can call her back and challenge her response, you have lost ground by your own lack of self-control. You have also set a very poor example.

> Do not make friends with a hot-tempered man,
>   do not associate with one easily angered,
> or you may learn his ways
>   and get yourself ensnared.
> (Proverbs 22:24–25)

It is harder, but more fruitful, to remain calm and have an honest discussion. Fights with teenagers, even if based on a real infringement, create more trouble than they are worth.

> A gentle answer turns away wrath,
>   but a harsh word stirs up anger.
> (Proverbs 15:1)

> A hot-tempered man stirs up dissension,
>   but a patient man calms a quarrel.
> (Proverbs 15:18)

Anger wastes an opportunity

So here is a mother who sets about the usual Saturday morning laundry. As she sorts it into piles, she notices with irritation that her teenage son's school uniform is absent. It is a house rule that uniform is put into the family laundry basket on a Friday night so that it can be washed, dried and ironed in preparation for the Monday morning. This is not the first time that this son has fallen short of this particular statute. The mother marches into the son's bedroom, where the son lies comatose under his duvet. Amongst the debris on the floor, she sees the offending articles. At this point it would be easy for her to collect them and add them to the piles of laundry. But the mother thinks to herself, 'I have done this before, and once too often. This boy is not learning to take responsibility. He has been disobedient and inconsiderate. If I pick up his clothes for him now, he will carry on his belief that it is always some woman's job to collect his clothes and launder them. One day perhaps he will marry (though on present viewing he is not much of a prospect) and his wife will wonder why his mother did everything for him . . .'

As the mother turns these and other thoughts over in her mind, she is irritated by her son's insouciant slumber; she fears for her son's slide into decadence and she responds with anger. She sweeps back the curtains to let in fierce morning sunlight, marches across to his bed and tears back the duvet. The tousle-headed boy blinks up at her in somnolent confusion. It is like a raid of the Gestapo. He hears his mother rant and demand his immediate rising to collect up one pair of trousers, one shirt, and some socks and boxers from the floor and place them onto a pile a few feet away. He complies, but he is outraged at the manner of this intervention. He cannot understand what all the fuss is about.

That mother was not wrong to be concerned at her son's aberration. He certainly needed to be taken to task. But when anger takes over, the opportunity for some real training is wasted.

> Better a patient man than a warrior,
>   a man who controls his temper than one who takes a city.
> (Proverbs 16:32)

> A fool gives full vent to his anger,
>   but a wise man keeps himself under control.
> (Proverbs 29:11)

If you want to win a battle with a teenager, you are more likely to do so if you are calm and patient.

Let us rewind the tape and allow that mother a second chance. How should she respond as a busy woman who wants to get the Saturday wash moving? She could make her son a cup of coffee and take it into his bedroom. Rousing him gently, she could wish him 'good morning' and explain *sotto voce* that she has woken him early because there is something important that he has omitted to do. Has he any idea what it might be? ('If you want a clue, take a look around the room.') She can then ask him politely to do what he should have done the previous evening. When he has done it, she can solemnly promise that his Saturday lie-in will be interrupted on a weekly basis, until he has learned this lesson for life.

In order to engage in this dialogue without clenched teeth, the mother will need to pray for a great deal of grace and patience.

Or she can consign him to dirty school uniform for the following week and let experience be his teacher.

Or she can collect up the laundry and make a mental note to engage her fully conscious son later that day in a serious conversation about the practical outworkings of the principle of consideration for others and the ongoing struggle with laziness.

There are options available. But experience taught me that losing my temper was the very worst.

Then again, you are well advised to choose your battles. Some things are best overlooked. Decide in advance which particular undesirable aspect of your teenager's behaviour you want to work on at any given time, and go for that one. Some words of correction have a later sell-by date. They will keep for another occasion.

A man's wisdom gives him patience;
  it is to his glory to overlook an offence.
(Proverbs 19:11)

Once again, we are directed to look for wisdom.

The answer to fear

The only ultimate answer to fear is faith. You do not know what will happen tomorrow, but you know someone who does. And he is a good God and your heavenly Father. As the old hymn says, 'His love is as great as his power, and knows neither measure nor end.'

Guilt and her babies

Just as we may have every reason to fear when we think about our children, so we may have many reasons to feel guilty. We feel guilty because we are guilty. Fear concerns the future, which is shrouded in the unknown. Guilt concerns the past, which has happened and cannot be changed. It concerns what we did and didn't do and what we said and didn't say.

At this point we ought to observe to ourselves that we do not have perfect recall. Nor do we unfailingly tell ourselves the truth about the past. So the guilt may be more or less than we think. But in some measure it will be deserved. The worst opinion that we or anyone might have of ourselves and our failings is in actual fact going to be better than the opinion we would deserve were all the deeds and motives of the past exposed. God is too kind to reveal all our sins to us at once. He knows it would be more than we could bear.

So we all suffer guilt. In regard to our children, we suffer the guilt of knowing that we could have done it better. And when we see in them characteristics which we deem to be the result of our parental failure, we suffer.

Sometimes, however, we do not tell ourselves the truth. The statement, 'My daughter would be a better pianist if I had made her practise more,' begs the question, 'Whose responsibility was it to practise the piano?' Your own practising at the keyboard would not have made her a better player, nor would your nagging in and of itself.

On the other hand, the statement, 'My son would have better table manners if I had taken the trouble to sit with him and teach him how to eat nicely,' might be true. We might be guilty as charged.

Where the guilt is real, the only solution is forgiveness. Jesus Christ deals with the actual guilt, not just the accompanying feelings. A Christian's daily prayer should include confession, contrition and the asking of God for forgiveness through Jesus. The relief gained from engaging in such confession is based on something real. The blood shed by Jesus on the cross really does take away the guilt.

But guilt spawns some nasty children. Here they are.

Guilt's bad baby number 1: Regret

Regret is what can linger even after the guilt has been taken away in Christ. It is pernicious because it is, like anxiety, a waste of energy. Regret has us saying things which begin with the words 'if only'.

A single parent, who became a Christian when her children were in their teens, realized that her children bore the consequences of her godless earlier life. 'If only I had become a Christian twenty years ago,' she said. 'I would have done things very differently.' But such contemplation is pointless. Don't go there.

There are three places you can go, however, if you find yourself drowning in regrets.

Firstly, you can use this admission of your past failure to know yourself more thoroughly. You are learning first-hand how dreadful sin is. This never does any of us any harm. Turn regret into repentance.

Secondly, you can embrace the forgiveness you have in Jesus Christ. The more we know our sins, the more truly thankful we are for a Saviour.

Thirdly, you can submit cheerfully to the sovereignty of God, which has brought you to this place. God has graciously given you time to change. So you can begin to sow a new harvest.

If these are not crocodile tears you are shedding, let your awareness of past mistakes give you courage in the present. The parents who truly regret buying a TV for their child's bedroom need to be brave enough to remove that TV and explain. This is a tough road, but it is an indication of real repentance, not mere sentimental regrets.

Regret is a bad baby because it paralyses us. It is the devil's tool because it tells us that nothing will be any good again. It is the road to despair.

Guilt's bad baby number 2: Surrender

Sometimes we like to try and compensate for our guilt. We use material things to make up, perhaps, for our neglect. We attempt to get our children onside by buying them things. These have the side effect of keeping our children out of our hair. If our children suspect that we buy them things to expiate our guilt, they are quite capable of exploiting us mercilessly. So, before we know it, our children have retreated to their rooms, to their PlayStations, their chatrooms, their mobiles, their iPods. These are the kinds of toys that parents buy to win their children's favour. It is an ineffective strategy, of course. It merely raises expectations and confirms a thankless child in the view that her parents only exist to supply her with 'stuff'. And too frequently, the very toys we buy distance our child from us.

Surrender means that the parents have given up. This may be a habit from when their children were little. Perhaps at that time they were misguidedly happy to hand their children over to virtual parents like TV. By the teenage years, these parents are surrendering very cheerfully, thinking that their work is done and encouraging their children to fend for themselves and explore all the avenues of 'normal' teenage behaviour.

Some parents surrender because they think it is pointless to fight. They continue to provide, but they no longer make the attempt to protect, instruct, direct or correct. If the music is too noisy, they shut their door. If their children's friends come round, they go out.

But the Bible would tell us to keep on the job. The game is not over. Our children are not ready to be let fully off the leash. However badly we think we have done so far, however weary we are, however much we just want a peaceful life, if we surrender now we are stopping short of the tape.

> Discipline your son, and he will give you peace;
>   he will bring delight to your soul.
> (Proverbs 29:17)

So the road to peace is not surrender, but discipline, which includes training, modelling, correction, instruction and encouragement – all those things. Remember that a teenager is unfinished business. He or she may yet bring delight to your soul, despite present appearances.

Guilt's bad baby number 3: Excess zeal

It is possible for parental guilt to metamorphose into an excess of zeal. Don't get me wrong. After-school activities can be excellent, as can be the range of sporting and musical courses and clubs on offer. But modern parents, eager to prove their excellence, can be over-eager to sign their offspring up for activities to fill every waking minute. Children, and especially teenagers, need time and space simply to muck about.

Some parents assuage their perception that they have been ineffective by attempting to become, in the teenage years, their child's best buddies. They almost become teenage themselves, affirming every teenage fad. They start talking the language; they effectively invade their child's world.

This is very bad news for the teenager, who will cringe with embarrassment if his Dad dons a baseball cap and starts attempting to do stunts on a skateboard in front of his friends. I recall old aunts (well, they were at least forty-five) attempting to do the Twist with us cool young things at family Christmas parties. Oh dear!

Your teenager needs his independent space, where he can begin to discover his identity apart from you. If you shadow him, he won't be able to do that. It won't help if you start emulating him in this unformed state.

This is also bad news for the parent. You hold a unique position in your child's life. Do not compromise it. Be flattered if your daughter borrows your clothes, but don't borrow hers. The Bible is very clear about preserving distinctives.

> Children's children are a crown to the aged,
>   and parents are the pride of their children.
>
> (Proverbs 17:6)

That verse paints a beautiful picture of family harmony. There is mutual love and respect. There is no call to paint on body glitter and invite your daughter to call you by your Christian name. The fact is that there is only one person in the whole universe whom she calls Mum and only one person she calls Dad. You hold a unique position. Use it as a platform from which to exercise sound influence. Let others be the groovy role models. You be Mum or Dad and hold your heads up. This is the way it was intended to be.

Why does it sometimes have to be so hard?
If it was intended for sinful, wobbling parents like us to have the huge responsibility of child-rearing, why is it frequently such a battle?

I counted taking my children out in the car for driving practice as one of the least pleasant duties of being a parent. Until they were competent at the wheel, it was a test of my nerve as well as my patience. As far as I was concerned, if there were a top ten list of the worst parental experiences, it was up there alongside potty training, or dealing with three travel-sick children throwing up in the back of the car.

Learning to drive, like learning to go to the loo in the right place, is a process that can take a long time. Any parent, any learner, would like to fast forward from lesson one to the hour of complete competence. But it cannot be done. Skills have to be learned and some boys and girls are slow learners, both in the use of the potty and in the handling of a motor car.

Longing for the finishing line
There are other times as a parent when you sigh and long for the *fait accompli*, the finishing line. You see some small, positive sign of spiritual interest and you ache for your teenager's conversion. You want it now, in case anything gets in the way.

Your son meets an excellent Christian girl and you long for an announcement and a ring. You want it signed and sealed. In the bag.

But we need to realize that these times when everything seems to be going in slo-mo are part of our story too. Let's not wish our lives away! Sometimes we feel as if we are watching a film of our teenager's life, waiting for a happy ending. We forget that we also are in the film. We not only have a part to play, we have a story. And these days of aching with longing, itching with impatience, sobbing with frustration and disappointment are part of our story. We too have a story and it consists, in part at least, of our responses to the challenges that raising a teenager brings.

While our children take their A levels, we may face a more serious test on the day the results come out. If our children fail to meet the standard required by the university of choice, will we fail to respond with gentleness, patience and submission to the sovereignty of God? Whether it is A levels or potty training, teaching to drive or clearing up vomit, the experiences which make up the twenty or so years of child-rearing can teach and train us. God uses these ordinary things in our lives to shape our characters. Sometimes he humbles us and makes us face our pride, envy or lack of self-control. Then he repeats the experience to see if we have learnt our lesson.

It is not only children who need to take correction well, in order to become wiser. We adults have that opportunity also. The point is, will we embrace it as such, or will we resent it?

> By wisdom a house is built,
>   and through understanding it is established;
> through knowledge its rooms are filled
>   with rare and beautiful treasures.
>
> (Proverbs 24:3–4)

For further thought or discussion

1. Why do we get upset when our children fail to reach our standards of taste or behaviour?

2. How can we turn from anxiety to prayer and praise?

3. When does discipline become control?

4. What are the trigger points for your anger with your teenager? Identify your fears.

5. How can guilt be good for us?

6. What makes a parent inclined to surrender?

7. What kind of lessons is parenthood teaching you? How is God using these experiences to make you more like Jesus?

8. Spend some time in prayer and thanksgiving over your children, naming your fears and confessing your guilt.

6. KEY STRATEGIES

Emily fumbled in her pocket for her keys. She had run all the way home in her high heels and could not wait to kick them off. It had been a dreadful evening. A few hours ago she had been getting dressed up, looking forward to the party and being with Tom, but it had all ended with a row. She had said some stupid things; he had said some cruel things. Now Tom would not like her any more. And she had made a fool of herself. Everyone had been drinking too much and behaving unpleasantly. In the end she had run off without saying goodbye . . . and now she felt sick and tired and miserable.

Finding her key, she stood in the porch and tried to slide it into the lock and turn it with minimal noise. Although she was only a few minutes after the 11.30 deadline, the house was in darkness.

Inside the front door, Emily kicked off her shoes. She caught sight of herself dimly in the hall mirror and was appalled. What a sight! In one way she was grateful that her parents were not still

> up to see her tear-stained face. In another way, she desperately
> wanted to talk to someone who would understand and comfort
> her.
>
> She tiptoed upstairs and hovered on the landing staring at her
> parents' closed bedroom door. Taking a deep breath, she walked
> up to the door and knocked timidly.
>
> 'Mum, are you awake? Can I talk to you?'

We are, by now, well aware that we will never be perfect parents. But we still have to be parents and we want to be the best parents we can be, without giving way to fear or guilt. How can we do that?

I have called this chapter 'Key strategies', but it is important to recognize right away that there is no formula to ensure that we get the desired result. There is no crib sheet, no book of answers. But there are wise priorities, and alongside praying for wisdom, we can pursue those wise priorities, which the Bible recommends for parents. These become our key strategies.

Key strategy 1: Screen the messages

All the time we and our children live and breathe on this earth, we receive messages. As we interact with others, as we read, listen and watch, ideas are being transmitted and exchanged. There is a little balloon which pops up on my computer whenever I switch it on, telling me that wireless networks are within the range of this computer. All I have to do, apparently, is to click on the icon. The writers of Proverbs were all too aware, even in those pre-electronic days, that human beings can pick up from a range of networks and not all of them are benign. There is the voice of wisdom:

> Does not wisdom call out?
>> Does not understanding raise her voice?
> On the heights along the way,
>> where the paths meet, she takes her stand;
> beside the gates leading into the city,
>> at the entrances, she cries aloud:
> 'To you, O men, I call out;
>> I raise my voice to all mankind . . .'
> (Proverbs 8:1–4)

But there is also the voice of folly:

> The woman Folly is loud;
>> she is undisciplined and without knowledge.
> She sits at the door of her house,
>> on a seat at the highest point of the city,
> calling out to those who pass by,
>> who go straight on their way.
> 'Let all who are simple come in here!'
>> she says to those who lack judgment.
> (Proverbs 9:13–16)

While commending the way of wisdom, Proverbs identifies some of the false and foolish messages that are out there and points out what lies behind them and where they lead. We do our children no favours when we pretend that those voices do not exist. They are loud and persuasive, like the woman Folly. Some Christians would like to create a parallel universe for their children, but such a universe does not exist. Rather, Proverbs encourages the parent to get acquainted with the messages. Screen the messages – by which I mean sort them out according to their desirability. We cannot delete them, but we can help our children to recognize them for what they are.

The presuppositions of Proverbs

If you think back to the biblical routes to wisdom outlined in chapter 4, you will realize that they are based on a rock-solid presupposition of absolute truth. Here wisdom speaks of herself:

> I was appointed from eternity,
>   from the beginning, before the world began.
> (Proverbs 8:23)

What was true yesterday is true today and for all time, because it corresponds to external reality. Truth and goodness remain, whether or not I subscribe to them. It is because these are eternal, unchanging truths that biblical faith is so robust. It is not wishful thinking, or a placebo to get us through the day. It offers something real to any who put out their hands and grasp it. It offers life as opposed to death. Again, wisdom speaks:

> For whoever finds me finds life
>   and receives favour from the LORD.
> But whoever fails to find me harms himself;
>   all who hate me love death.
> (Proverbs 8:35–36)

There are, however, many voices who would now argue against any kind of absolute ultimate realities of this kind. They would call it arrogant and insensitive to talk in these black-and-white terms. They would suggest that we all find our own personal truth. These voices are not merely in university faculties of philosophy, but in prime-time chat shows and the words of a rap.

It is entirely possible to demonstrate to anyone who will listen that the doctrine which denies the existence of absolutes is untenable, illogical and ultimately self-defeating. After all, Professor A's statement that all truth is relative is in itself a proposition which is relative and therefore not worthy of one second of my consideration. Professor A is wasting his breath. But meanwhile, putting that objection and others like it aside (for that is the subject of another book), we as parents must engage with our offspring who are being exposed to the mantras of postmodernism through every available window. What shall we do?

First of all, we can make it our business to know what those mantras are. What follows is a list of some of the most current messages of the world we all inhabit.

'Good is what I decide it shall be'

This demonstrates an utter lack of conviction, a complete absence of consistency.

> At the window of my house
>> I looked out through the lattice.
> I saw among the simple,
>> I noticed among the young men,
>> a youth who lacked judgment.
> (Proverbs 7:6–7)

This lack of judgment is not confined to callow and impressionable youths. It is espoused by those in the highest intellectual circles, where lacking judgment has become a virtue. You see it every weekend in the supplements of the more upmarket newspapers, where the shallow, tawdry and degenerate are frequently celebrated for breaking taboos and being unconventional in the name of art or fashion.

According to this gospel, the ultimate virtue is to be non-judgmental, even where any fool might see that boundaries

of good taste and good behaviour have been crossed. The
truth is that any fool has seen fair and called it foul, and foul
and called it fair.

> A fool finds pleasure in evil conduct,
>   but a man of understanding delights in wisdom.
> (Proverbs 10:23)

By this kind of relativism, any behaviour is defensible. The
writer of Proverbs knew about it too, referring to the kind of
person who robs his father and mother and says, 'It's not
wrong' (Proverbs 28:24). In contrast to this destructive folly,
there is the wisdom based on the revelation of the eternal
Creator. It is established and unchanging, full of joy and life,
and available to all who will listen.

> Blessed is the man who listens to me,
>   watching daily at my doors,
>   waiting at my doorway.
> (Proverbs 8:34)

'What's in it for me?'
A generation of young people have been systematically
trained to ask that question. Indefatigably entertained by
their parents, bribed into acceptable behaviour, they are
largely ignorant of such old-fashioned virtues as unselfish-
ness, loyalty and service. Even love, although approved of
theoretically, is in danger of becoming merely self-serving.

This kind of individualism is almost impossible to counter
within an atheistic worldview. On the other hand, the Bible
commends the two great, inseparably linked commands to
love God and love your neighbour as absolutely the best way
to live.

Let love and faithfulness never leave you;
   bind them around your neck,
   write them on the tablet of your heart.
Then you will win favour and a good name
   in the sight of God and man.
(Proverbs 3:3–4)

There is a reward for those who pursue virtue, but the reward is neither material nor sensual. It is a reward with a Godward focus. Those whose lives are driven by individualism are denied the delight which only those who love unselfishly have discovered.

'As long as I feel OK, I am OK'

This saying translates in a teenage world as, 'As long as my peer group approve and affirm me, I am OK. Otherwise not!'

It is hardly surprising that bullying in school is apparently at epidemic proportions. I am aware that cruelty between children is an issue worthy of the most serious attention. But I also observe that children are now raised to be acutely sensitized to the approval / disapproval of others. Their fragile egos can sometimes turn them into affirmation junkies, so a cruel text message or an indifferent sneer can lead them to despair. In a different way, this rampant emotionalism is evident from a brief glance down a school corridor between periods. Many secondary school teachers these days are complaining that pupils are late for lessons because so much time is being spent in hugging each other. An absence of hugs is a bad day. Equally, standing up for what is right might expose you to the almost unbearable censure of your peers. Admitting that you got it wrong, or owning up to a misdemeanour, would be extremely uncomfortable. It wouldn't feel nice, so don't do it. That is the argument of emotionalism.

Fools mock at making amends for sin.

(Proverbs 14:9)

'Today's pleasure is worth tomorrow's pain'

At a trivial level, it is this kind of thinking which leads a teenage boy to remove the uneaten pork pie from yesterday's lunchbox and leave it mouldering on a shelf in his bedroom, only to be found weeks later by a disgusted older sister with a more sensitive nose. Teenagers are sometimes incapable of thinking ahead.

But this 'presentism' can be seen at a more serious level. How else can you explain the folly of young girls who engage in one-off sexual encounters with boys they barely know, let alone like? The tragic evidence is that many young women make this same mistake quite knowingly again and again. The consequence is often an unwanted pregnancy, followed by an abortion, followed by a repetition of the whole cycle. Or, choosing to keep the baby, not necessarily out of any respect for another human life but out of an ill-tutored emotionalism, this young woman is set for a life of poverty and abuse at the hands of feckless or brutal young men. None of these consequences comes as a surprise to the unfortunate girl in the case; it is not knowledge she lacks, but the ability to live for anything but the present.

Proverbs describes a similarly foolish young man, being tempted to sexual adventures with a married woman, as one who lacks judgment. Trouble certainly awaits him.

Can a man scoop fire into his lap
    without his clothes being burned?
Can a man walk on hot coals
    without his feet being scorched?

. . . a man who commits adultery lacks judgment;
 whoever does so destroys himself.
Blows and disgrace are his lot,
 and his shame will never be wiped away.
(Proverbs 6:27–28, 32–33)

The same 'presentism' is what prevents a responsible attitude to assignments:

A little sleep, a little slumber,
 a little folding of the hands to rest –
and poverty will come on you like a bandit
 and scarcity like an armed man.
(Proverbs 6:10–11)

Teenagers are particularly vulnerable to this danger. The ability to plan ahead and strategize is itself a mark of maturity. I recall as a teenager thinking I would never be old; it was impossible to imagine even being thirty! A teenager is well and truly bound up in what is happening in her little world right now and needs help to look down the track.

It is worth noting that the philosophy of 'presentism' is the precise opposite of the 'no gain without pain' idea which has permeated orthodox Christian discipleship down the centuries. For the Christian, the eternal perspective is crucial. It is through many hardships that we enter the kingdom of God. A course of action may appear easy and pleasant, but be wrong; the wicked may live in a house, an apparently stable structure, while the upright have only a tent, but it is the house not the tent that will fall.

The house of the wicked will be destroyed,
 but the tent of the upright will flourish.

There is a way that seems right to a man,
> but in the end it leads to death.
(Proverbs 14:11–12)

'I have to have that to be happy'

Materialism is so central to our way of life that we barely notice it. In the developed world we all have more than we need or use. Even comparatively less well-off families will spend hundreds of pounds on Christmas presents for their children, giving credence to the lie that things can make you happy. Or if not things, then a certain appearance. For teenagers this might mean having a certain style and brand of footwear. There is massive importance attached to how you look and what you wear. There are also certain accessories deemed to be 'essential' kit. Phones, which do a hundred different things, iPods and other high-tech gizmos are as much sought after for how they make the owner look as for any value attached to their functions. The father in Proverbs warns his son about getting in with a crowd who love stuff, or 'plunder'.

> . . . we will get all sorts of valuable things
> and fill our houses with plunder . . .
(Proverbs 1:13)

Some young people are particularly drawn to an affluent lifestyle: the clothes, the cars, the luxuries. These things can prove to be a snare. They are inherently deceitful because they never deliver. The father warns his son not to crave the delicacies of the rich man, and Proverbs' last words reinforce the point that beauty and charm are temporary, while godliness with contentment is great gain.

Charm is deceptive, and beauty is fleeting;
　　but a woman who fears the LORD is to be praised.
(Proverbs 31:30)

'It's not my fault'

So entranced is our society by the myth of high self-esteem, that we are all extremely adroit at blaming others for anything that goes wrong. If we are late, it is the fault of the person who could have woken us up; if we drink too much, it is the fault of the person who was handing it out; if we are rude, it is the fault of the one who provoked us, and so on. Not that this is a new human phenomenon; it was going on in the garden of Eden.

But this age-old human habit of looking for someone to blame has reached dizzy heights of professionalism within a culture which enjoys suing for damages and medicalizing every human failing. This is excellent! We can blame other people for everything that goes wrong and may even be financially compensated. At the same time we ourselves are untouchable, for when the finger points at us, we were not bad, just unwell. We were depressed or traumatized or stressed and could not help our errant behaviour.

This 'victimism' is in the air we breathe. Small wonder that teenagers find it hard to take responsibility for their choice of action! Sometimes their parents are all too ready to make excuses for them – and be assured, the teenager is quick to catch on. Not that he needs any help. The dog who ate the homework is part of the mythology of the staffroom. In the days of Proverbs it was the fault of the lion in the street.

The sluggard says, 'There is a lion in the road,
　　a fierce lion roaming the streets!'
(Proverbs 26:13)

The Bible, however, is quite clear about responsibility before God.

> Rescue those being led away to death;
>> hold back those staggering towards slaughter.
> If you say, 'But we knew nothing about this,'
>> does not he who weighs the heart perceive it?
> Does not he who guards your life know it?
>> Will he not repay each person according to what he has
>> done?
> (Proverbs 24:11–12)

'You cannot be serious'

The fashionable postmodern thing to do with truth is to debunk it. Make fun of it, make merry or distract from its power with a cynical remark. This is the common way to meet the claims of Christianity. Young people will be encouraged to investigate *feng shui*, crystals, meditation, paganism or even the existence of fairies, but they will be taught to assume that Christianity could not be true. 'No right-thinking, intelligent person could possibly believe in a creator God.' And, 'Isn't religion the cause of all the trouble in the world?' It is interesting and alarming to note that God takes this dismissal out of hand very seriously.

> Then they will call to me but I will not answer;
>> they will look for me but will not find me.
> Since they hated knowledge
>> and did not choose to fear the LORD . . .
> (Proverbs 1:28–29)

God calls us to submission to his revealed truth and ultimately to himself. This indeed is the beginning of wisdom.

What shall a Christian parent do?

All of the above is a searing indictment of our culture. I do not intend to trash every product of every medium of the last few decades and accuse them of propagating undiluted error. There are, of course, songs, TV programmes, films, educational ideas and so on which buck the trend. Unbelievers sometimes spot the hollowness or hypocrisy of contemporary secularism and rightly mock or challenge it. Christians do not have the monopoly on truth, and truth is truth wherever it is spoken. All truth is God's truth. By God's common grace, things are not as bad as they might be. But they are bad enough from the point of view of a Christian parent, who is trying to raise a teenager at this point in history.

The old axiom that the bad will destroy the good unless the good is defended is one of which Christian parents must remind themselves on a daily basis. Defending and confirming the gospel is the job of every Christian parent. And you cannot defend against an enemy you do not know. That is why I have outlined the lies of secularism at some length. We must understand the world our young people inhabit.

In 1960, Penguin Books were prosecuted under the newly amended obscenity laws for the publication of D. H. Lawrence's *Lady Chatterley's Lover*. It became a *cause célèbre* and notable men and women of letters queued up to speak for the defence of the book. The case for the prosecution, led by Mervyn Griffith-Jones, was that writers, artists and publishers had a responsibility to consider what the effects of their work were likely to be. If this work could be published, surely anything could be published. Was it in the public interest that all restraints on publication be lifted? It was an important question worthy of very serious consideration, but Griffith-Jones made some critical errors in his speech which more or less sealed the case for the defence. He said, 'Ask yourself this question . . . would you approve of your young sons, your daughters – because girls can read as well as boys – reading this book? Is it a book you would leave lying about your house? Is it a book you would even wish your wife and servants to read?'

The court burst into peals of laughter. How could anything said by anyone so ridiculously out of touch be taken seriously? And so a critical test case was lost; the floodgates of permissiveness were opened.

Christian parents must not make the same mistake. They must correctly identify the lies. They must defend the truth in a way that is relevant to the rising generation.

Practical points

Although this key strategy may seem philosophical and theoretical, it most definitely is not. Here are some things that every parent can actually do.

- Read books and newsapapers, watch TV and films *with* your children and spot lies. Discuss issues.
- Be careful to maintain biblical input via family prayers, personal Bible reading and church. This input should encompass all Christian truth.
- Discuss the Sunday sermons. Relate what you learn from the Bible to current events, personal or national.
- Consider reading together some Christian apologetics – C. S. Lewis, Francis Schaeffer, Josh McDowell.
- Introduce the family (or let them introduce you) to some good, contemporary Christian music, songs which defend and confirm faith.
- Invite your children to introduce you to something they consider good. Then discuss its truth or otherwise.

- Maintain your children's involvement in worthwhile Christian activities. Make it a given that they attend church and all that your local church offers for young people. When, spiritually, our children were at their lowest ebb, their friends at church kept them within earshot of Christian wisdom.

The biblical worldview is refreshingly liberating. Do your children understand that? Do you?

Key strategy 2: Strengthen the relationship

None of the practical suggestions outlined above will be open to you unless you are maintaining a warm relationship with your teenager. Sometimes parents seem to me to be almost frightened of their teenage children. They make known their dislike of their teenager's music, habits and dress sense and effectively promote 'no-go' areas in the home and 'keep out' notices on the bedroom door.

This is the very opposite of what you want as a parent, which is to keep all channels of communication open. You may doubt this, but it is better to hear their music, than not hear it because you have soundproofed their bedroom.

I am not saying there is no place for discipline and correction in the teenage years, but they will not work unless there is open communication and a warm relationship. Rules without relationship lead to rebellion. You know it is true.

So keep working on your relationship through all the shifting patterns of your child's growth and development. A relationship is never static. It needs attention and maintenance.

The insecurity of the teenage years cannot be overstated. Because teenagers frequently feel unlovely, they need more than ever to know that they are loved by their parents. Now, that love has to be appropriately expressed. Hugs and kisses may meet resistance, but physical contact is important. A friendly touch as you pass can carry an important message. Eye contact can be hard work and many teenagers studiously avoid it, but make it your aim always to meet their eyes when you speak to them. It is immensely affirming to meet the eyes of someone who genuinely loves you.

Keep the regular windows of communication open

What is the regular window for communication and relationship with the various members of your family? It is the family meal table.

We all know the significance of going out for a meal with someone: it is less about the food, and more about the sensation of being together, the opportunity for some uninterrupted conversation. That is why going out for dinner has always been the best kind of date. And this is thoroughly biblical. Think about the significance of 'eating with' in Scripture. It conveys a message of belonging and acceptance. From the Passover to the Lord's Supper, from Jesus eating with tax-collectors and sinners to his description of himself standing at the door in Laodicea and hoping to be invited in, eating together has huge significance for relationship. And for families it is the easiest and most natural of resources. We all have to eat. Yet it is widely reported that these days many children are not eating with their parents. A study in March 2000, reported in *The Archives of Family Medicine*, found that of 16,000 school-age children questioned, less than half ate with their parents on a daily basis. I suspect that the percentage continues to fall. In March 2008, at the annual conference of the Association of School and College Leaders, John Dunford, the general secretary, made a speech concerning the demise of the traditional family and the detrimental effect of that demise on the behaviour, attitudes and achievements of today's schoolchildren. He described a generation of children who are increasingly relying on teachers to become surrogate parents. He said, 'In relation to the family, one of the most important factors has been the loss of the family meal, which has reduced family conversation so that schools have more to do in teaching children to communicate.'

Now the current concern with childhood obesity tells us that these children are not starving, so what are these young people doing? They are snacking, or, as it is termed, 'grazing', while standing by the fridge; they are taking their plates to eat in front of the television; they are eating in their bedrooms. Not only is this bad for their physical health and the development of social skills, it is a travesty of what family life could and should be. It is also woeful neglect of a precious daily opportunity for communication.

The value of eating together

The family meal table is of particular value during the teenage years, because once it is established as a routine, it provides a built-in opportunity for seeing your children without making an appointment. You are all checking in with each other in an informal way. Just expect your children to be in for meals and plan to eat together, all of you, round a table as often as possible. Of course there will be occasional absences for good reasons, but make sure that the pattern is there, a pattern that works. The demands of salaried employment may make it impossible for both parents to be present on a daily basis. In which case, one parent must be careful to keep the routine going and sit down *with* the children. Do not let this habit drop. Want to be there. Expect them to be there. It is much easier to talk over food, far less intense and threatening, far more friendly.

The family meal table is inclusive: an intrinsic message of acceptance and belonging, common identity, shared life, shared work, shared joys and sorrows. A meal together is a great opportunity for wisdom, not via a lecture, but through stories, news, comment, discussion and evaluation of the day's activities, current events, plans, dilemmas, successes and failures, perhaps Bible reading and prayer. It is a time for perspective. It is a time for being real and warm, for healing wounds, for saying in the most difficult times that things may be bad, but we are still together and God has faithfully provided for our needs.

So don't be too busy to set the table and serve something tasty, sharing together in the pleasure of food. It need not be elaborate; in fact, simple is good. Beans on toast is the elixir of the gods when eaten in cheerful company.

> Better a meal of vegetables where there is love
>   than a fattened calf with hatred.
> (Proverbs 15:17)

Mind your language
Teenagers are acutely sensitive – it goes with the insecurity about the childhood they are leaving behind and the adulthood they are about to enter but feel so ill-equipped for. Proverbs emphasizes again and again the impact that speech has on people.

> Reckless words pierce like a sword,
>   but the tongue of the wise brings healing.
> (Proverbs 12:18)

It reminds us of the importance of tone of voice:

> A gentle answer turns away wrath,
>   but a harsh word stirs up anger.
> (Proverbs 15:1)

It commends knowing when to shut up:

> A man of knowledge uses words with restraint,
>   and a man of understanding is even-tempered.

> Even a fool is thought wise if he keeps silent,
>   and discerning if he holds his tongue.
> (Proverbs 17:27–28)

These skills are critical for the parent of a teenager. How often have I 'gone off on one' and made everything worse! How often have I made a sharp or sarcastic remark and seen the look of anger in a teenager's eyes! On the other hand, how fruitful has been a word of kindness.

> An anxious heart weighs a man down,
>   but a kind word cheers him up.
> (Proverbs 12:25)

These skills are particularly necessary when you want to correct or challenge behaviour.

> Through patience a ruler can be persuaded,
>   and a gentle tongue can break a bone.
> (Proverbs 25:15)

Parents of teenagers frequently get the impression that whatever they say is wrong. If they try to be nice, they are accused of being patronizing and get a prickly response. If they say nothing, they don't care. If they make a helpful suggestion, they cause offence. The book of Proverbs knows all about that, because it knows that as a parent of a teenager you are dealing with a fool.

Do not answer a fool according to his folly,
    or you will be like him yourself.

Answer a fool according to his folly,
    or he will be wise in his own eyes.
(Proverbs 26:4–5)

These two proverbs help us to understand the proverb genre. Tremper Longman III writes in his commentary that 'Proverbs are not universally true laws but circumstantially relevant principles.' Whether or not you engage with a fool, or indeed a teenager, depends on the nature of that fool or teenager and the general context. But of course, whatever you decide to do, you are likely to get it wrong.

Don't poke the monkey

Your teenage daughter appears at breakfast with a sour look, her head down. You try to ignore it and go for bluff cheerfulness, but meet with a blank stare, a deep sigh, or even an angry 'What's your point?' Recall these two gems:

If a man loudly blesses his neighbour early in the morning,
    it will be taken as a curse.
(Proverbs 27:14)

Like one who takes away a garment on a cold day,
    or like vinegar poured on soda,
    is one who sings songs to a heavy heart.
(Proverbs 25:20)

My husband and I had a saying to each other for such breakfast times: 'Don't poke the monkey.' Pretend not to notice. This may be a good time to pick up the newspaper.

The message and the meta-message

You need to be aware of the meta-message. This is the underlying, or even overarching, message which, although unspoken, is actually clearer than the words that are said. What we say and what we mean are not the same. Teenagers are well aware of that. What we mean to say and what we are understood to mean are not the same thing either. Even an innocent question is received by a teenager as a statement of disapproval. Often what angers a daughter is not the kind of information a mother's question seeks, but the judgment it seeks to imply.

'Are you going out like that?' is not, let's face it, just a question.

This can happen with an apparently insignificant exchange of details as much as with more emotionally laden talk. Sometimes we just need to learn to say less. Choose battles you can win. Ask fewer questions. Teenagers hate an inquisition:

'How did the day go?'
'What happened today?'
'Did you have a good time?'
'Who was there?'

But maintain a relationship where information will, if you are patient and non-threatening, be freely imparted. Be available, but not in their face.

Many parents have discovered the value of driving a teenager somewhere alone in the car. Because the parent is driving and therefore unable to look at, let alone poke, the monkey, the monkey sometimes starts to talk.

In the story with which this chapter commenced, Emily would not have disturbed her parents' sleep for what turned out to be a crucial and fruitful interchange, if she had not had confidence in her mother's unconditional love. Teenagers do not tend to risk rejection. The trust relationship must be pre-established over years of not seeming to do anything very significant.

Find common ground

Without embarrassing your kids by trying to perform an 'ollie' on a skateboard, it is really helpful to find things you can enjoy together. These pastimes may be short-lived, so don't go and buy all the expensive equipment and then gnash your teeth to see it gathering dust in the cupboard under the stairs. Here are some ideas:

- Stories, TV programmes or films
- Music or theatre – try out a band, orchestra, musical, circus or Shakespeare
- Sport, whether kicking a ball in the park together or engaging in some collective spectating – going to watch a match is a great bonding experience, even when it is sharing misery when your team loses, again
- Games, whether electronic or old-fashioned board games
- Cooking – invite them to provide the meal one night a week, and offer to be their kitchen slave
- Clothes – do a trawl of the charity shops together
- Active exercise – running, biking, rowing, climbing, skating, tennis – exhausting but good

You may have to undertake some of these things under cover of darkness, or while you are on holiday, where your teenager will not be spotted by his friends. That also is OK. Go with that and make no comment. Be the kind of people your teenager (at least when his peers are not watching) is comfortable around: safe, dependable, unchanging and unmistakeably on his side. Be as familiar as an old coat, as dependable as Marks and Spencer, as loyal as Lassie.

Key strategy 3: Spotlight the heart

Too often as parents we have been satisfied, not to say relieved, if our children appear to be doing the right thing. What we fear most is being exposed as parents; we fear the censure of other parents, other church members. So we have concentrated on externals, because if our children look good, then we look good. Your teenagers may well expose and trash those idols.

So we congratulate ourselves that we don't allow our children to go clubbing, but never question what they are doing in all those hours on the computer.

Proverbs again and again stresses the importance of the inner life. It is the man of perverse *heart* that the Lord detests. It is the son's *heart* which has to be kept on the right path.

> The LORD detests men of perverse heart . . .
> (Proverbs 11:20)

> Listen, my son, and be wise,
>   and keep your heart on the right path.
> (Proverbs 23:19)

The sexual abstinence movement (for example 'True Love Waits') which has gained considerable ground in the United States in recent years is in many ways an excellent and commendable thing. Naturally, any Christian parents would want their teenager to save sex for marriage. But to focus specifically on a rule and behavioural prohibition might just miss the point. The problem, in this area of vulnerability as with all the others, is in the heart. It has to do with idols. That is why, in addition to warning his son about the inadvisability and unhappy consequences of illicit sex, the father in Proverbs spends so much time commending wisdom. 'Where is your heart?' That is the question we must always be asking our children, implicitly or explicitly. Otherwise their acceptable outward behaviour is just the gold ring in the pig's snout (Proverbs 11:22). The pig is still a pig.

God's values and ours

We can be very easily satisfied and even unconsciously encourage a worldly attitude in our children. How dare we accuse our children of succumbing to peer group pressure? Are we more interested in our children getting top grades at A level than in their attitude, for example, to money? Are we more concerned about the clothes our children wear than the attitude behind the choice? Are we satisfied if our daughter doesn't get pregnant, but unconcerned that her heart is full of lust?

Are our values really God's values? Our priorities must be heart priorities. In matters of discipline, it is essential to appeal to the conscience. When correcting, it should be character issues that concern us, for example laziness, rather than the fact of a poor mark for an assignment.

It is essential for a child to recognize that the essence of the problem is always his own heart. Parents can be tempted to lower standards to enable their children to be able to keep them. That is not the Bible's way. On the contrary, the Bible's point is that the wise thing to do is to recognize our failure and downright inability to keep God's standards. That is why we need Jesus. This thought should never be far away in our training and discipline of our children.

That does not mean that we never encourage our teenagers. Far from it! But the encouragement must be in the context of our learning and growing, rather than having achieved. Apart from using the means of communication and routes to wisdom outlined above and in earlier chapters, one thing we can do is to praise our children less for outward things and more for inward things. It is good to pay your son a compliment when he has taken trouble to scrub up, but a generous action or a patient attitude is more worthy of positive reinforcement, as is a wise choice or an honest response.

> An honest answer
>   is like a kiss on the lips.
> (Proverbs 24:26)

Key strategy 4: Shape dependence on God

> The wisdom of the prudent is to give thought to their ways,
>   but the folly of fools is deception.
>
> Fools mock at making amends for sin,
>   but goodwill is found among the upright.
> (Proverbs 14:8–9)

Teenagers are generally aware that their parents are not perfect. It is important for your teenager to know that you too are cognisant of your own imperfections. 'All sinners here' should be freely and frequently acknowledged. Be quite open about your own journey and the struggles it entails. In a situation where you, the parent, are challenging or correcting your offspring about some undesirable attitude or behaviour, it can be immensely helpful to admit that the struggle with sin is one in which you too are engaged.

Acknowledge your own failure and weakness
It is a mark of a fool not to admit a fault. Model to your children what to do when you know you are at fault. Virtue

includes the acknowledgment of failure and the need for atonement. We miss opportunities with our teenagers when we pretend to be right all the time.

Also they will see what we are and be disappointed in our hypocrisy.

So be honest, because that will help them to be the same. An example of this kind of honesty and admission of human frailty is in Proverbs 30.

> 'I am the most ignorant of men;
>> I do not have a man's understanding.
> I have not learned wisdom,
>> nor have I knowledge of the Holy One.
> Who has gone up to heaven and come down?
>> Who has gathered up the wind in the hollow of his hands?
> Who has wrapped up the waters in his cloak?
>> Who has established all the ends of the earth?
> What is his name, and the name of his son?
>> Tell me if you know!
>
> 'Every word of God is flawless;
>> he is a shield to those who take refuge in him.
> Do not add to his words,
>> or he will rebuke you and prove you a liar.'
> (Proverbs 30:2–6)

As Tremper Longman comments, here we have 'strong religious affirmation on the heels of a frank confession of human frailty'. It would be so foolish in commending wisdom to pretend to be all-wise yourself. The book which began with a parent exhorting and pleading with his son to pursue the promise of wisdom, is coming to a close with an acknowledgment of the limitations of the human mind, an awe in the presence of the Creator and an encouragement in the midst of human ignorance to avail oneself of God's flawless words.

This is the question we must ask ourselves. Where will our children run? We want to shape a dependence on God's words, not our own. It is those that will enable them to find refuge in time of trouble. It is this that will enable them to find true identity in Christ.

Our children need to see us taking Scripture seriously, reading it, meditating on it, memorizing it, letting it colour our conversation and lifestyle.

Our children need to find us at prayer, admitting our weakness, failure and dependence. They need to witness us, in the troubles which ambush us, running to God and walking humbly with him. This is an important perspective, because it is true. Although throughout our children's lives to date, we parents have been able to solve most of their problems, they will pretty soon meet situations which are beyond the handling of a mere parent. Ultimately you do not want your children to run to you, but to God. He will be there when you are not. He is utterly dependable, while you – yes, even you – may let them down. He keeps all his promises; you merely do your best. Many things are out of your control, but they are not out of his.

This is the perspective, then, with which to raise teenagers: the perspective which goes from a tent to a fortress.

> The house of the wicked will be destroyed,
>   but the tent of the upright will flourish.
> (Proverbs 14:11)

The house would appear to be a pretty stable structure, but it will be demolished, while the tent, moving on with God, not encumbered too much with this world, will prosper.

He who fears the LORD has a secure fortress,
  and for his children it will be a refuge.
(Proverbs 14:26)

Parents who place themselves in a proper position with regard to the Lord, recognizing that it is not about them but about him, are under his protection. And who knows when their children will run to that refuge? Perhaps for some years they will treat the idea of needing a fortress with some disdain. But the protection will extend to them too, on the day they recognize their peril. Then they will start running for the place which proved such a safe haven for their parents.

For further thought or discussion

1. Why can a parent not create a parallel universe for his child, a kind of sterile bubble free from untoward influences?

2. Which of the messages are current in the thinking of your teenager or his/her associates? How will you counter them?

3. Why is it that a relationship with a teenager can be so much more difficult than one with a younger child?

4. What can you do to make family meal times a cheerful focal point for family life? Why is it important to do so?

5. In what ways do our words pierce like a sword? What kind of words bring healing?

6. What obstacles are there to finding common ground with a teenager? Think about what you can do from your side to remove those obstacles.

7. Why are we so much more comfortable with making external prohibitions than with attempting to deal with the heart? Why is it important that we spotlight the heart?

8. In what ways are you modelling and commending dependence on God's word?

9. Why is God's word more important than your word?

7. WHEN DREAM TURNS TO NIGHTMARE

Debbie was delighted when Paul, the sixteen-year-old son of one of the elders, offered to babysit so that she could go to the midweek meeting of the church every Wednesday. As a new Christian and single parent of two young children, she really relished the opportunity this gave her to learn more about the Bible and to spend time with other Christians. For his part, Paul said he would appreciate the quiet house and a couple of undisturbed hours to do his studying. Debbie made sure the children were tucked up and asleep before she left. She would return at about 10pm to find Paul with his head down over the textbooks spread over the dining table.

This mutually beneficial arrangement continued for a couple of months. Then, one Wednesday evening in winter, Debbie came over rather shivery while at the Bible study. So, instead of staying for a time of more questions and sharing, over coffee and biscuits, she made her excuses and left. It was just after 9pm when she let herself through the front door. Immediately she noticed that

> *things were different. There was music and the sound of voices,*
> *murmuring and giggling.*
>
> *Surprised, Debbie walked into the sitting room. 'Has a friend*
> *come to . . .' she began, but stopped as her question was completed*
> *and answered. Her aghast gaze took it all in: low lights, clothing*
> *on the floor, Paul and a young nymphette on the sofa, unclothed,*
> *turning their heads to return her stare, wide eyed and red faced.*

If you find the above scenario offensive and consider that your offspring could never engage in such disgraceful behaviour, then, fair enough, skip on to chapter 8. But I write not only as one who has raised teenagers and has observed teenage behaviour, but as one who *was* a teenager and remembers. And I have read the Bible.

The Bible, as we have seen, knows all about the temptations of the teenage years; it also understands the feelings of the wayward teenager's parents.

> A foolish son brings grief to his father
>   and bitterness to the one who bore him.
> (Proverbs 17:25)

In the aftermath of the events described above, it was not merely Paul's behaviour which shocked and grieved his parents, it was Paul's duplicity. Another father told me with tears that it was all those lies his daughter told him which had wounded him the most. Loving parents think they know their children; it is their instinct to trust them. Parents are understandably angry and hurt at the systematic betrayal of that trust, sometimes over a long period of time.

There is a delightful and imaginative picture book by the children's writer and illustrator John Burningham. Entitled

Would You Rather?, it invites the reader on every page to choose from a range of scenarios, graphically and humorously depicted. Would you rather be made to eat spider stew, slug dumplings, mashed worms or drink snail squash? Would you rather an elephant drank your bathwater, an eagle stole your dinner, a pig tried on your clothes or a hippo slept in your bed? Little children giggle and shout 'Yuk!' or 'No!' at each pictorially presented option.

Suppose there were such a book created for the parents of teenagers. Would you rather . . .

- your son was caught *in flagrante delicto* (see above)?
- your daughter was out, almost clothed, drinking and clubbing every Friday and Saturday night until 2am?
- your son was caught using crack cocaine?
- your daughter was bulimic and a self-harmer?
- your son declared that he was gay?
- your daughter was arrested for shoplifting?
- your son lived a godless but respectable life as an accountant?

As with the choice between slug dumplings and spider stew, you might find yourself recoiling from any of these scenarios. Or perhaps not. Perhaps you see the choice as easy: you would take the last option. But actually, all of the above are demonstrations of folly, godlessness as much as drunkenness. In fact, godlessness is at the root of all of the above. The more acceptable manifestations of godlessness are not ultimately less painful and heartbreaking than the more shocking ones.

Of what use is money in the hand of a fool,
    since he has no desire to get wisdom?
(Proverbs 17:16)

To have a fool for a son brings grief;
    there is no joy for the father of a fool.
(Proverbs 17:21)

In fact, remember the rich young man whom Jesus loved (Mark 10:17–23). He was a fine, decent-living boy, the kind of son any mother might have been proud of, but his possessions set him further from the kingdom of God than the many prostitutes, tax-collectors and general losers with whom Jesus regularly associated. There may be respectability in riches and earthly status, but there is no comfort there. Many believing mothers and fathers of godless but respectable adults understandably break their hearts every night over their offspring who have walked away from Jesus. We must look at things the way Jesus did. He knew it was certainly not 'game over' because a person had made some idiotic choices and landed up in a mess.

The point of the 'would you rather?' exercise is that comparisons are pointless. We all make them. We say, 'I would rather she had . . .' but we are wasting our mental and emotional energy. We must face it: we do not have a choice, and if we did have a choice we would probably choose badly.

There is a way that seems right to a man,
    but in the end it leads to death.
(Proverbs 16:25)

We do not have the control and we do not have all the facts. But God does. So let him decide. His providences may sometimes be bewildering, but God's sovereignty is a safer and saner option than yours or mine.

Many are the plans in a man's heart,
    but it is the LORD's purpose that prevails.
(Proverbs 19:21)

There is no wisdom, no insight, no plan
    that can succeed against the LORD.
(Proverbs 21:30)

There doesn't have to be a reason

OK, so as parents we accept that we do not choose our teenager's brand of folly, but surely there must be a reason why they are behaving in such an awkward, wayward, forward, backward way?

Here are some of the reasons that various parents I have spoken to have offered for their teenager's rebellious and miscreant behaviour.

- We were too strict.
- Our lifestyle was too narrow.
- He/she got in with a bad crowd.
- We gave her too much freedom.
- We focused too much on externals.
- We were too gullible.
- The school did not keep us informed.
- The church was very negative and critical.
- We were too involved in work/church/other ministries.

These things may or may not be objectively true. I cannot judge and neither should any other outsider. Obviously they cannot all be true in any particular case, because some are contradictory. Parents in this situation are, by definition, racked with guilt and on the lookout for someone to blame, whether themselves or a third party.

Teenagers who take a walk on the wild side may also cite reasons. These are among those I have heard.

- I felt I was not part of the family.
- I was fed up with being treated like a two-year-old.
- I didn't appreciate being told what to do.
- Church was old-fashioned and boring.
- The people at church didn't like me.
- I wanted to be the same as my friends.
- I was adopted and needed to find myself.
- Everybody else was doing it.
- It's just what you do. No-one said it was wrong.
- It's my life.

Again, although these views may be sincerely held, they may or may not be objectively true. The reasons may be invalid, morally and logically. And again teenagers are also affected by guilt and the need to blame, generally, someone else.

But perhaps there doesn't have to be a reason. There are certainly no one-to-one correlations, say, between strict upbringing and taking drugs, or busy/absent parents and teenage pregnancy. The above list is an excellent demonstration of parental and teenage frailty, but does not particularly aid our understanding.

Possible factors

Where true, those things the parents mention undoubtedly make their unhelpful contribution. The Bible neither defends nor exonerates judgmental Christians or neglectful parents, but those things make the impact they do because of the particular vulnerabilities of an individual young person. And where there are those vulnerabilities, the young person doesn't need narrow-minded parents as an excuse. He can go wrong all by himself. That is why young people with loving, fair-minded and sensible parents sometimes get into serious scrapes.

> Even a child is known by his actions,
>   by whether his conduct is pure and right.
> (Proverbs 20:11)

We are back in chapter 3 with fools, mockers and simpletons. I will not reiterate, except to say that of particular potency when a child chooses the wrong path is the role of friends. One wounded father said, 'Friends were everything – I cannot emphasize that too strongly.' Even conditions and behaviours that seem to have an individual, psychological basis, like anorexia or self-harm (and I am by no means minimizing their desperate nature), do not happen in isolation. A school nurse told me, 'These things come in clusters, almost fashions. If I see one self-harmer in a school, I know that very soon I will see several more in the same school.'

That is why the first practical subject that the author of Proverbs tackles with his son is the temptation to go along with the crowd.

> My son, if sinners entice you,
>   do not give in to them.
> (Proverbs 1:10)

One underlying cause

The underlying cause is the folly of teenagers. At the risk of being repetitious, I maintain that the Bible's view is that folly is the default position of teenagers. The book of Proverbs is not afraid to repeat that the inability to take advice or correction is the insurmountable roadblock on the route to wisdom.

A mother told me that her daughter refused to attend the church youth group after one of the leaders challenged her attitude. 'She could not take criticism,' said the mother, sadly. 'After that she set her heart against church and did her own thing.'

Whoever loves discipline loves knowledge,
   but he who hates correction is stupid.
(Proverbs 12:1)

Listen to advice and accept instruction,
   and in the end you will be wise.
(Proverbs 19:20)

Prevention – always achievable with hindsight!

Many parents say they did not see disaster coming; some admit to being completely taken in by the double life their children led. In such cases, how could they prevent it? I humbly offer the earlier chapters of this book as a general preventative medicine. Unfortunately, the laboratory conditions do not exist in which to test their efficacy scientifically. On the causes and cure of the more bizarre teenage problems like bulimia, anorexia and self-harm, I can pretend no expertise. The reader must look elsewhere for that and discover that on these subjects even experts do not necessarily agree.

Prevention in hindsight is by definition theoretical. 'If only . . .' is a game to play only if you focus on your own behaviour and intend to change it. All the other variables are out of your control. So, instead of talking in 'if only' terms, the rest of this chapter will play the ball from where it is. Here you are; it is ghastly; what shall a parent do?

The smorgasbord of emotion – you do have a choice
A parent's initial response to a teenager in freefall is emotional. In general, the first emotions are negative and very powerful. Psychologically, emotions give the parents energy and drive to keep going. They become a way of surviving. But the Bible warns us about hanging on too long to negative emotions. They can become a way of life and be hard to lose because, as Paul explained to the Ephesian church with reference to anger, they give Satan a foothold on your life (Ephesians 4:26–27). Instead, the biblical principle is to replace a negative with a positive, for example:

> Do not say, 'I'll pay you back for this wrong!'
>   Wait for the LORD, and he will deliver you.
> (Proverbs 20:22)

In the following list of parental emotional responses, a healthier alternative will be suggested in every case. I am not in any way saying that this is easy. This may be a daily struggle, on your knees before the prayer-answering God. But:

> An upright man gives thought to his ways.
> (Proverbs 21:29)

- Anger and resentment: *'How could you do this to me?'* The very question exposes the first concern here, which is for the parent's own reputation. Instead ask God to stir compassion in you.
- Disappointment: *'After all that we taught you . . .'* Choose instead meekness. Humble yourselves under God's mighty hand.
- Embarrassment: *'What will the neighbours think?'* Instead, let God be your judge. Bring everything before him in

prayer. That will deliver you from the tyranny of other people's criticism.

- Self-pity: *'I am just going to sit at home and cry.'* Instead, choose thankfulness. Thankfulness that now you know, you can pray and act. Thankfulness that God holds the future.
- Grief: *'I could have handled his/her death better than this.'* Extreme teenage rebellion is a kind of bereavement. You grieve for the loss of the dreams you had for what your child might become. Choose to let those dreams go.
- Guilt: *'This must be my fault.'* Instead confess your sins and embrace God's forgiveness.
- Fear: *'What will become of him/her?'* Choose instead to trust the Lord.

He who conceals his sins does not prosper,
   but whoever confesses and renounces them finds mercy.

Blessed is the man who always fears the LORD,
   but he who hardens his heart falls into trouble.
(Proverbs 28:13–14)

Have no fear of sudden disaster
   or of the ruin that overtakes the wicked,
for the LORD will be your confidence
   and will keep your foot from being snared.
(Proverbs 3:25–26)

Love's austere and lonely offices

Emotions are what drive you, but what behaviour should a parent choose? How do you actually live with a foolish son and daughter? In a poignant poem entitled 'Those Winter Sundays', Robert Hayden coined the phrase 'love's austere and lonely offices' in recalling his own father, getting up early to light a fire in a cold house and to polish his awkward and ungrateful son's shoes. No-one ever thanked him; his teenage son responded with indifference. 'What did I know,' Hayden reflects, 'of love's austere and lonely offices?'

It can feel distressingly lonely to be the parent of a wayward teenager. You look around and see everybody else's children doing the accepted thing. You suffer the real or imagined condemnation of your peers. But still there are things you must do, out of love and faithfulness to your child, even though he will not thank you. It requires the same kind of commitment and self-discipline as getting up and lighting a fire in a cold house.

> What a man desires is unfailing love.
>
> (Proverbs 19:22)

A parent in this position does not always feel very loving. Hence the austerity. But what is required is dogged perseverance. So here are some of love's austere and lonely offices.

Keep praying

Andrew and Nicky (not their real names) are Christian parents whose lives during their two daughters' teenage years were beset by the utmost misery. Both girls had been happy, high-achieving children at primary school. Their elder daughter became moody and difficult at the age of thirteen and then turned increasingly errant and uncontrollable. Aged sixteen, she left home, encouraged by a dangerous and violent boyfriend. She went to the social services office. Their verdict was that the relationship with her family had broken down and they gave her the money to move out. The boyfriend abused and mistreated their daughter. The spiral of problems continued with other unhealthy relationships.

Andrew's and Nicky's younger daughter had also been talented and well-motivated. But she contracted a very serious eating disorder, which almost claimed her life. Nicky recalls her daughter sitting by a radiator in her pyjamas, and 'there was nothing there; she was a blank cardboard cut-out'.

Andrew and Nicky talk extensively about the importance of prayer through these long and lonely weeks, months and years. This is what they say.

- Look to God, not other Christians, because they may not be supportive.
- Don't be afraid to admit you have a problem and ask your Christian church family to pray.
- Don't blame God. You may feel abandoned, but you are not. He understands and he is the perfect Father.
- Ask the Holy Spirit to apply the wisdom of God to your heart and mind. He is all-seeing and all-knowing.
- Work together with your husband/wife. Teenagers are devious and will try to play you off against each other.
- Pray *together* about the children/problems.
- God knows how you feel, so it won't surprise him if you shout at him about how you feel. I (Nicky) had sessions in the conservatory, shouting out at God.
- Never feel that all is lost.

Keep watching (at a distance)

Andrew and Nicky speak of the feeling of helplessness they had. That is the objective reality. There comes a point at which there is nothing you can do but pray and watch what happens. But remember that learning from experiences is a route to wisdom. That is why it is important to let your teenager experience the consequence of his errant behaviour. Even if you could protect him from it, it is better not to do so. This is tough love indeed. I talked to parents who called the police when their (drug-taking) son was violent at home. It was better that he saw where the road he was taking was leading. It would not have helped to mend the furniture and say nothing. The same parents learned to be meticulous about not making any cash available to their son.

But while a parent is watching, that parent is not indifferent. Here love's austere and lonely offices may include provision of food and clothing, or accompanying your child to court.

If a child is involved with outside agencies, for example for counselling, do not besiege her with questions when she comes home.

Keep in touch

If the teenager is still living at home, it is important to establish a mutually agreed set of rules. Here again, choose a battle you can win. A pastor and his wife wanted to continue to offer hospitality, even though their teenage son had become openly hostile to the church and anything remotely Christian. They told him that at certain limited agreed times, their home would be open to church members and that he, the son, could absent himself at those times if he wished. On the other hand, he was welcome to join them for meals. But there would be no 'room service'.

Aim in general to eat together as a family every day, even if those meals are strained. Pretend not to notice. Keep up the family routines of checking in with each other. If a child has left home, find a way to hang in with her. Nicky met with her daughter sometimes in town, sometimes by visiting her in her flat. She and Andrew were determined to keep in contact, even though their daughter neither asked for such contact, nor received it graciously. However, she did occasionally call in at home for food or hugs.

These times of contact are important, but painful. They call for immense patience and self-control. Many times Andrew and Nicky came away from seeing their daughter and wept.

Keep your own rules
It is obviously important at any stage of life and in any company to avoid hypocrisy and practise what you preach. But with a mistrustful, resentful teenager who is looking for evidence that you don't care or that your standards are unreasonable, it is crucial that you live by those things you have stood for.

Continue to pursue all those spiritual disciplines, such as reading, memorizing and meditating on Scripture, which you have built into your lives over the years.

> For the LORD gives wisdom,
>   and from his mouth come knowledge and understanding.
> He holds victory in store for the upright,
>   he is a shield to those whose walk is blameless,
> for he guards the course of the just
>   and protects the way of his faithful ones.
> (Proverbs 2:6–8)

Let love and faithfulness never leave you. If you have commended calmness, reasonableness and self-control, then you must demonstrate it, even though you have to grip your hands firmly behind your back and take several very deep breaths before you speak. Do not underestimate the difficulty of this. Many parents, who passionately love their miscreant offspring, speak of the fury which all but overwhelms them at times. Pray for grace.

Stone is heavy and sand a burden,
  but provocation by a fool is heavier than both.
(Proverbs 27:3)

Some temptations to handle

Love's austere and lonely offices can make the parent vulnerable: vulnerable to invidious comparisons with other parents,
vulnerable to exhaustion and despondency, vulnerable to a
loss of faith in other people. So here, based on what those
who have suffered with their teenagers have told me, are
three 'no-nos'.

- *Don't cite other people's children* – not to yourself and not,
  especially not, to your own teenager. Everyone is
  different; everyone has a different story. Learn not only
  to weep with those who weep, but also to rejoice with
  those who rejoice.
- *Don't spend all your time on this problem.* Of course, that is
  easier said than done, when you feel you are on 24-hour
  watch, but even then, for your own sanity, mentally find
  somewhere else to go. Read, paint, dig the garden, help
  a neighbour, do your work, walk, swim, embroider.
  This will help you keep your sanity as well as a good
  perspective.
- *Don't hide yourself away.* This is a very real temptation,
  because you fear being asked about your son or
  daughter. But on the contrary, this is the time to find
  who your real friends are. Give them a chance. They
  will get it wrong some of the time, but forgive and
  forbear. Many parents who have come through this
  experience (or who are still going through it) talk of
  the value of a having a small circle of people (or
  maybe only one person) with whom they can be

totally honest. One mother I know has permission to call a particular friend at any time and ask for prayer, which is sometimes shared then and there over the phone.

A friend loves at all times,
   and a brother is born for adversity.
(Proverbs 17:17)

A man of many companions may come to ruin,
   but there is a friend who sticks closer than a brother.
(Proverbs 18:24)

What about the future?

There is no knowing how long, under God's sovereign purposes, you, the wounded parent, will be called upon to watch and pray in this way. I cannot give you a timescale. So how do you proceed with what seems like an ongoing situation? There may be progress on some fronts, because with maturity your teenager may 'calm down' a little. But even where there is a mellowing of the relationship between you, thanks to the grace of God and your unremitting pursuance of those austere and lonely offices, there may be scars. There may be 'issues'.

As the teenage years come to an end, all parents should be working themselves out of the job of being parents and into a relationship of friendship. Friendship works on the premise of acceptance. So, when a son or daughter has walked a path you wanted them to avoid, you have to build a relationship on the basis of what he or she is now. Put aside the cherished hopes you had for them years back. Get to know this person now. Present realities have to be squarely faced and embraced.

Andrew and Nicky now enjoy a warm and positive relationship with both their daughters, even though their life-styles are in some respects 'alternative' and not everything is resolved. Of their older daughter they write:

> We have learnt to build relationships with H's friends and boyfriends in order to get to know them better as people. H has appreciated this and the support and encouragement we have been able to give. We have not necessarily liked or had a lot in common with some of them. Praying for them and their needs and problems has helped. It has surprised us that we have ended up liking and enjoying spending time with some very 'different' people.

A great day

For Andrew and his elder daughter, this was the day they were reconciled – a prodigal returning moment.

> She travelled alone with me in the car to visit my mother. I shared the love and pain I felt very honestly and she opened up completely – we both cried driving along in the car – a wonderful moment. It was probably when I first realized she had never stopped loving and respecting us and had maintained a walk with God through it all.
>
> I think of her as a 'Samson' – who would want to cope with him as a son? And yet God saw him as a man of faith.

For further thought or discussion

1. How does the Bible's view of human nature help when things go wrong?

2. Why do we value 'respectable' godlessness?

3. What reasons do we give for our child's wayward behaviour? Are they valid? Is there anything within our power which we ought to change?

4. Why does our children's misbehaviour make us furious?

5. Which of love's austere and lonely offices do you consider most important? Why?

6. How does Andrew's and Nicky's story encourage you?

7. How would you advise and support the shocked and discouraged parents of Paul (from the story at the beginning of the chapter)?

8. How could Christian friends help you as a wounded parent? What would such friendship require of you?

9. Name a scenario you dread for your youngster. Commit it to God now.

8. MORE THAN SURVIVAL

It was a sunny morning during the summer holidays. I selected a pair of cheery cropped trousers and put them on, frowning at myself doubtfully in the mirror. I'd had them a few years.

When Owen made his appearance at the breakfast table, I stood up and said to him, 'What about these trousers? Is it still all right to wear these?'

Owen paused in the pouring out of his Frosties and took a long look at me, head on one side. His face broke into a slow smile.

'They're OK, Mum. But then, it's not like you've got any street-cred to lose!'

As I complete the writing of this book, my youngest son (introduced above) is turning twenty, a teenager no longer. Since he is the last, by some years, of my brood of four, I have always been aware that the passing of every phase of his development was the end of an era for me. For some of these passings I did not mourn. It was with a sense of celebration that I accepted the fact that I would never again be responsible for the potty training of a child. I am also glad to have no further truck with GCSEs, A levels or interminable parents' evenings. But even so, having a teenager in the house, *that* I will miss. There may have been some storms and scowls and plenty of smelly trainers in the hall, but for me these have been the very best of parenting years.

I say that because teenagers in general get a very bad press, and even in this book I have been candid about the very real potential for disaster. I have taken up the Bible's description of teenagers as fools, mockers and simpletons, not with intent to insult or abuse, but in order to clarify the baseline. But there is more that can be said about teenagers. In my experience, under that hoodie, behind that eye make-up, there frequently lurks a human being of immense charm, affection and wit.

In my experience, under that hoodie, behind that eye make-up, there frequently lurks a human being of immense charm, affection and wit.

This book is written in the hope that parents will do more than merely survive the teenage years. I hope they will relish them, look back on them with pleasure and use them as the foundation for something lasting and excellent in the future.

Affection

The incident recounted above was a turning point in my relationship with my youngest son. It was the day I recognized that I could relate to him as a friend and, more crucially, that he could reciprocate. The remark he made regarding my appearance would at an earlier stage of life had been considered impudent and he would have been rebuked for it. But in that incident at the breakfast table, a new dynamic was revealed. Owen unconsciously claimed his right to tease me, to expose *my* folly. Who, after all, was acting like a teenager in that situation – the sixteen-year-old boy or the fifty-something woman?

The experience of discovering a friend in one of your offspring can only be described as delightful. In our house it crept on in every case from the middle of the teenage years. In some families it may be later. It is encouraged by shared interests: sport in the case of our boys; Jane Austen with our daughter. It is evidenced in small conversations or shared moments, by in-jokes or sudden flashes of utmost honesty. It may be captured in tears, but even more in laughter as you recognize alongside your children your equal frailty as human beings. And you discover that this kind of relationship has huge healing properties all round. Ordinary affection carries a family through.

> Hatred stirs up dissension,
>   but love covers over all wrongs.
> (Proverbs 10:12)

You start to see a shift in roles. You find yourself asking your son or daughter for assistance in mundane things like reaching a top shelf or reading a map. You find that on both sides you are glad to have each other around to share in the adventure of life. Do not underestimate the power and comfort of ordinary affection. Do not be afraid to show it (in appropriate and unembarrassing ways).

Stimulation

It is now a cliché, the superior technological know-how of the rising generation. It is through our children that we discovered texting, downloading, buying on eBay, booking online, even (way back) setting the video recorder. The fearless optimism of youth when faced with something unfamiliar is wonderful to behold and I have often been grateful for it. Our children have not allowed us to stay in the twentieth century; they refused to accept our learned incompetence. They frog-marched us into brave new worlds.

Nor has this stimulation been merely technological. More importantly it has been cultural and intellectual. We might have remained unchallenged in our opinion that the music actually did die when The Beatles split up, had our children not introduced us to Oasis, U2 and Coldplay. All right, there was plenty of dross on the way, but what fun we had arguing about it! And an S Club 7 routine was very good exercise for the middle-aged Mama (in the privacy of the kitchen, obviously).

Provided there is built-in space and permission for it, teenagers also keep their parents on their toes intellectually, ethically and theologically.

'Dad, why does the Bible speak of the unchanging God as changing his mind?'

'Mum, one of my friends has told me he is gay. What should I say?'

'How does Richard Dawkins get away with it? Is he right when he lays all the evils of the world at the feet of religion?'

'What is a fundamentalist? Is it always a bad thing?'

These are the kinds of discussions which can occur over shepherd's pie on a Monday evening. What a relief to have moved on from 'Use your spoon, Owen' and the Swapshop book of 1,000 best jokes to pulling down the strongholds of secularism! Just imagine that: pulling down a stronghold at your own dining table.

A wise man attacks the city of the mighty
　　and pulls down the stronghold in which they trust.
(Proverbs 21:22)

As iron sharpens iron,
　　so one man sharpens another.
(Proverbs 27:17)

Finally, stimulation can be social. Your children will introduce you, not formally of course, to other teenagers. Some of these you may only get to know by their first names or an extraordinary sobriquet like Buzz, Squid or Doppo, but who knows, you may make a new friend! You may be able to exercise some positive, if subtle and unacknowledged, influence on their lives. Perhaps you may find some of these friends challenging, but delight in the fact that God has brought across your path a range of different people whom otherwise you would never have met. Get to know them. Try to understand them. Love them.

Not all stimulation is heavy duty. Teenagers, once they are past the monosyllabic grunting stage, are a fount of witty and entertaining repartee. Let them entertain you.

A cheerful heart is good medicine . . .
(Proverbs 17:22)

Education

The road to wisdom may be a long and painful one for your teenager. But, in most cases, they do get there. They may not seem to be accepting your input. They may seem to be blind to the obvious connection between, say, laziness and failure. You may have to watch your teenager make really stupid choices and bear the consequences. But the good news is that in many, many cases they do learn. They may not admit it to you for years, but they do learn.

A TV documentary in 2008 followed the progress of a charismatic musician and choral specialist, Gareth Malone, in his attempt to get the boys of a Leicester comprehensive school to sing. *The Choir: Boys Don't Sing* was the title of the series and the opinion of the vast majority of pupils and teachers at this school. But eventually, sing they did, thanks to Gareth's belief, hard work and inspirational leadership, and possibly the presence of television cameras.

One boy, Imran, was a very interesting case. He was gifted with one of the best natural singing voices in the school. Gareth began giving personal tuition, but Imran was a classic 'can't take correction' teenager. He couldn't be bothered. He stropped out. He responded to Gareth with insults and abuse. But Gareth's patience won him back. Imran finally listened, and performed his solo, to tumultuous applause, at the Albert Hall. And across the nation viewers on their sofas reached for the tissues. They were moved not merely by his singing, but by Imran's own comment afterwards: 'Don't be an idiot when people try to help you. I'm ashamed that was me.' The mocker had gone. Imran was on the road to wisdom.

> Drive out the mocker, and out goes strife;
>> quarrels and insults are ended.
> (Proverbs 22:10)

> If you are wise, your wisdom will reward you;
>> if you are a mocker, you alone will suffer.
> (Proverbs 9:12)

The wisdom of tradition, based on the experience of years, will also come to be respected. From the making of a lasagne to the buying of a house, a young person finally realizes that his parent is a pretty useful source of advice. Education is about knowing how to ask the right question and being unafraid to approach the person best equipped to supply an answer.

Cooperation

One aspect of raising teenagers that this book has largely omitted so far is the beneficial role of other people. We are all too aware of the capacity for harm of a subversive peer group. But peer pressure can work the other way and all kinds of people, of varying ages, can have a positive impact on your child's life.

It is of tremendous benefit for a teenager to have a Christian peer group. Or, even if they are not yet all converted, it is immensely supportive to associate with a group of people who are steadily and regularly under gospel influence and whose lifestyles are wholesome and generally honest. Such groups can be found in the youth work of many evangelical churches. Of course, from the earliest years you the parent have to give the message that this is the best possible scene to be part of. You must be a church-first family. Attendance at such groups must be an unquestioned feature in the family diary. Other commitments are optional, but not this one. A teenager who grows up with such a group of friends can count himself lucky. Encourage and expect your teenager to go, even if he or she seems initially unwilling. Pretend not to notice. Don't ask whether they enjoyed it.

Some Christian families are committed to small churches where there are few young people of their children's age. It is obviously harder in such a case for a young person to find Christian peers. Perhaps there is a like-minded church a short distance away which has a youth work to which your teenager could be affiliated. Additionally, there are many youth camps which offer opportunities for wholesome activity, solid Bible teaching and strong friendships.

Adults, apart from parents, can also have a very valuable input into a teenager's life. A young person can reap great benefit from the friendship or particular interest of a range of adults in the church or in the family. Such people are generally cooler and better dressed than the teenager's own parents, but even when they are not, a teenager may respond well to the kind overtures of any trustworthy adult who is willing to have an open home or put out the hand of friendship.

When our daughter transferred her membership from the church she had grown up in to a church in the town where she and her husband had settled, she wrote a letter to the elders of our church. In it she mentioned a range of people who had had a subconscious but significant impact on her life through their patience, instruction, example, interest and prayers, especially during her teenage years. She recognized that at times she had been challenging, moody and unresponsive, but these folk had shown true Christian forbearance and love. So take a bow: Bible class teachers, youth leaders, aunts, uncles, godparents, grandparents and kind church members everywhere.

He who walks with the wise grows wise.
(Proverbs 13:20)

As a parent, it is helpful to acknowledge that raising a child has a community aspect.

Sanctification
Don't be too hasty to get the teenage years over and done with. They are part of your story too. And they are of great

worth in your own progress towards holiness. The Bible is quite clear that one purpose of suffering is to produce character and perseverance in the believer's life (Romans 5:3–4). If you suffer at the hands of your teenager, and many parents do in one way or another, then you can know that God has organized this for your training. There are lessons to be learned in the school of patience, kindness, gentleness and self-control. These are lessons that would not be learned if you were raising a perfectly biddable, hard-working, tidy, punctual, polite, considerate and ever-cheerful teenager. So God gives you someone moody and scruffy to live in your house.

The first thing you discover is that you are not as joyful, patient, kind and self-controlled as you thought you were. You get a D minus at the first test. Then God presents you with the same situation again to see if you have learned anything.

The next thing you discover, perhaps after repeated failure, is that you need help. That is precisely what your heavenly Teacher wanted you to learn. He wants you to recognize that, like Agur, son of Jakeh, you 'have not learned wisdom' (Proverbs 30:3), but that:

> Every word of God is flawless;
>   he is a shield to those who take refuge in him.
> (Proverbs 30:5)

God gives you several years in this training school, and, by the time your child is twenty, if you have been able to take God's correction and discipline, you will be further along the road to sanctification than you were eight years previously.

It is not just your offspring who must walk God's routes to wisdom.

He who trusts in himself is a fool,
    but he who walks in wisdom is kept safe.
(Proverbs 28:26)

Gratification

The pleasure of family is among the highest joys this life can offer. Reciprocated affection, mutual acceptance and understanding between generations of a family are huge common grace blessings.

For a Christian parent, there is something even greater to hope and pray for. That is the day on which your son or daughter speaks of being safe for eternity through trust in Jesus Christ. One father told me of the day he met his son from a train journey and saw immediately that things were different. 'Dad,' said the son, 'I'm going to tell you something you have been waiting years to hear.'

It is an indescribably wonderful thing when you discover that your refuge has become their refuge. They have discovered the secret! When the children in C. S. Lewis's *The Lion, the Witch and the Wardrobe* tell the professor of their adventures in Narnia, they recognize that Narnia is something they will forever have in common. Once a king in Narnia, always a king in Narnia. A shared love of God's wisdom is a continuing shared joy.

A man who loves wisdom brings joy to his father.
(Proverbs 29:3)

All your instruction has been in the fervent hope that your children will trust the Lord for themselves.

Apply your heart to what I teach,
    for it is pleasing when you keep them in your heart

and have all of them ready on your lips.
So that your trust may be in the LORD,
   I teach you today, even you.
(Proverbs 22:17–19)

You will have the gratification of hearing truth from your children's lips which you didn't put there. Sometimes they will talk more wisely than you. Sometimes they will challenge your own spirituality. This is God's work and an immense and poignant joy.

My son, if your heart is wise,
   then my heart will be glad;
my inmost being will rejoice
   when your lips speak what is right.
(Proverbs 23:15–16)

You will have the gratification of knowing that your training and discipline were not in vain. Some periods of your child-rearing were sheer, thankless hard work. Perhaps you saw other parents settling for a quieter life, just saying 'yes', giving up, opting out. Perhaps you feared that your child would hate you for sticking to what you believed in and maintaining standards. But you stayed on the case and now enjoy both peace and delight.

Discipline your son, and he will give you peace;
   he will bring delight to your soul.
(Proverbs 29:17)

You will have the gratification of being vindicated before a watching world. There are many who want to say that a solid Christian upbringing messes children up. But although there are those teenagers who seriously rebel and go off the rails, this is by no means the norm. Children raised by loving Christian parents according to biblical guidelines are secure and stable, equipped for taking their place and making their contribution in an insecure and unstable world. Having been loved, they can offer love. Knowing their significance as created by God, they treat themselves and others with respect. Without being perfect, they make reliable employees, employers, citizens, colleagues, neighbours, friends, husbands, wives and parents.

To an average observer, my own children are unremarkable. They have won no prizes; they have ordinary jobs. And yet I have found to my surprise that our non-Christian friends and family members find them in some way impressive. I detect in their comments something approaching envy that all four of them should have turned out so regular, so comfortable in their skins, so decent, so thoroughly pleasant. 'Do you mean they got married without shacking up together first? How quaint!' And they laugh, but more from the wonder of it. They recognize that it is fine and beautiful. We feel vindicated. And we believe that God is glorified. For indeed, he has done it.

Be wise, my son, and bring joy to my heart;
    then I can answer anyone who treats me with contempt.
(Proverbs 27:11)

Succession

There is something more important than my own well-being and gratification as a parent. And that is the work that God is doing in the world throughout human history. God's plan is that one generation of his people should by training and instruction pass on the baton of truth to the next. Each

Christian family is a repository for truth. As one generation succeeds another, that truth is handed on.

We have already faced the fact that we cannot instil faith in our offspring. Faith is God's gift. But by your teaching, example and prayers, you the Christian parent have a God-given, vital role to play. Your commendation of God's truth is the best inheritance you can give your children, which they in turn can pass on to theirs.

> A good man leaves an inheritance for his children's children.
> (Proverbs 13:22)

In God's economy, respect and mutual pride are shared across generations. Children, of any age, are to honour and delight in their parents. Those parents, in old age, take delight in a new generation.

> Children's children are a crown to the aged,
>   and parents are the pride of their children.
> (Proverbs 17:6)

No-one is sidelined. The young are valued for their strength and energy, the elderly for their wisdom and grey hair.

> The glory of young men is their strength,
>   grey hair the splendour of the old.
> (Proverbs 20:29)

Succession, of course, depends on marriage and progeny. The book of Proverbs, which has so much in the way of advice to the young, ends with a mother emphasizing to her son the importance of marrying well. Next to the decision to follow Jesus Christ, the most crucial choice anyone makes in life is whom to marry. The nub of the advice in Proverbs 31 is 'don't go for money', because noble character is worth more than rubies, and 'don't go for cute'.

> Charm is deceptive, and beauty is fleeting;
>> but a woman who fears the LORD is to be praised.
> (Proverbs 31:30)

There we are again, right back at the beginning: the importance above everything of fearing the Lord. It is the very beginning of wisdom. It is the characteristic, above all, to spot in a potential marriage partner. Find a girl who fears the Lord; be a girl who fears the Lord.

This is what will secure the succession which is more than survival. So the generations, under God's gracious hand, roll on until Jesus returns. This God-fearing couple in their turn will raise their family with the predominant aim that their children too will get wisdom. And in the strength and dignity of that God-fearing young woman's old age, her children in turn will rise up and bless her.

> Many women do noble things,
>> but you surpass them all.
> (Proverbs 31:29)

It seems an ordinary thing to raise children. It is certainly commonplace. But where it is successfully accomplished, where healthy, wise, God-fearing young adults are launched to take their place in the world, to love God and their neighbour and to perpetuate and live out God's truth, it is a surpassing achievement which honours our God and Saviour and brings its own exquisite reward.

For further thought or discussion

1. When does an impudent remark become a friendly tease?

2. What are you enjoying about the teenage years?

3. In what ways are you stimulated by your teenage children? What is there that you need to learn from the rising generation?

4. What other adults have input into your child's life? Is there a way to thank and encourage them?

5. How can you make a positive difference to a teenager who is unrelated to you?

6. What lessons are the teenage years teaching you?

7. What inheritance do you have to leave your children?

8. What has raising children to do with God's plans for the world?

9. Spend some time praying that you and your children will do more than survive the teenage years.

APPENDIX: FOR FURTHER READING

> *Car window stickers:*
>
> *You can always tell a teenager . . . but you can't tell him much.*
>
> *Employ a teenager . . . while he still knows everything.*

I am well aware that I do not know everything about teenagers and how to bring them up. What I do know, I have largely learned from others. There are many, many books on this subject and I have not read even a fraction of them. What follows is a list of some I have read and found very helpful. I commend them to any reader who has an appetite for more.

Commentary on Proverbs
Tremper Longman III (Baker)
I have read a number of worthwhile commentaries on Proverbs, but I consider this one to be outstanding. Of particular merit is the lengthy introduction explaining the genre of Proverbs, and comparing and contrasting other ancient texts of similar ilk. It is a technical commentary and if you are, like me, utterly ignorant of Hebrew, you will just have to

take Tremper's word for it and move on. I found this commentary to be worth the perseverance.

This is not a book for the train, nor for the faint-hearted, but it is one to expand the mind. This is the book that set me onto the routes to wisdom. For a learned commentary, it is surprisingly contemporary and warm.

Aren't They Lovely When They're Asleep?
Ann Benton (**Christian Focus**)

Forgive the immodesty, but I still think this is a useful little book. C. S. Lewis said that when he wrote the Narnia stories he wrote the kind of books he would have enjoyed as a child. I wrote the kind of book on raising children that I would have liked to have read as a young mother: short, practical, biblical and set in a world I recognized. You can read it in half an hour. It will not insult you with too much detail, nor bore you with endless repetition. People tell me they have found its principles helpful.

Shepherding a Child's Heart
Tedd Tripp (**Shepherd Press**)

This is probably most relevant to parents starting out with young children, but it also makes helpful reference to the teenage years. Tripp is superb on how to discipline in a way that deals with heart issues. I read this book after my own book was published and was ecstatic to discover another speaker/writer on parenting who saw the folly, indeed crime, of bribing children to behave well. Since bribery is recommended as the strategy of choice in all kinds of behaviour management contexts (even some Christian ones) and is the point over which I have received the most hostile questioning over the years, it was wonderful to read someone who takes that whole ethos and puts it through the biblical shredder. So if you are in any doubt, read Tripp and then tear up those ghastly charts.

Age of Opportunity
Paul David Tripp (**Presbyterian and Reformed**)

A lengthy but readable book, this is a thorough guide to hand-ling the teenage years. Culturally it is firmly set in the US, so there are obvious differences. But I loved Tripp's exposé of differing modes of Christian child-rearing, via his description of the Smiths and the Joneses. His analysis of the different messages picked up by teenage radar is truly excellent. I leaned heavily on it for part of chapter 6 of this book.

World-Proof Your Kids
Tim Sisemore (**Christian Focus**)

Although I take issue with Dr Sisemore's expectation of fruit of the Spirit from those who, although born to believ-ing parents, are not born of the Spirit, there is much to commend this book. It is certainly one to challenge parents who expect their children to be more godly than they them-selves are.

Each chapter studies a fruit of the Spirit. The list of prac-tical suggestions at the close of each chapter (including suggestions for teens) is very good indeed. And I love the way the whole self-esteem thing gets a good slapping.

Why Do They Do That?
Nick Pollard (**Lion Publishing**)

This is an entertaining and enlightening read about the teenage subculture. It is written by a man whose personal experience from years of working with teenagers has helped him to understand their world. It quotes relevant research and is itself eminently quotable. That is where I found the amusing sayings from car window stickers given at the beginning of this appendix.

I Kissed Dating Goodbye
Joshua Harris (Multnomah Publishers)

A bit of a joke in our family because of all those stories he tells. Just how many girls did Joshua Harris kiss before he kissed dating goodbye? Nevertheless, he makes a good case. If you can get your teenager to read it (now that *might* require a bribe), and you read it yourself, you will have an excellent discussion starter.

Preparing for Adolescence
James Dobson (Regal Books)

Old-fashioned, but still true. We read this *with* our children before they were teenagers. We laughed together at the cheesy and dated bits, but still learned something. The chapter on peer pressure was, and is, timely and crucial.

Bringing Home the Prodigals
Rob Parsons (Hodder and Stoughton)

This book has been an immense help and encouragement to many who grieve for children who have walked out on the faith or on the family. It is a tear-jerker, so be warned. But it engenders hope and lets those who suffer in this way know that they are not alone.

Puppet on a String
Helena Wilkinson (Kainos Trust)

A book about anorexia by someone who has been there. It is one of the few books which say that anorexics can recover. Kainos Trust also offers support to sufferers and their parents.

Secret Scars
Abigail Robson (Authentic Media)
This autobiography helped me to understand something of what goes on inside the head of a self-harmer who was also anorexic and bulimic. The appendix detailing organizations which may be able to help could also prove to be a useful resource.

The Cutting Edge
Jess Wilson (Authentic Media)
On the same subject as the above, but a book you could give to a self-harmer who is also a professing Christian. It includes some practical suggestions for a way forward and is helpfully God-centred.

Growing up . . . growing wise@home
Lovewise (www.lovewise.org.uk)
This is an organization which creates, distributes and presents materials for sex education. It is of a high quality and promotes a biblical view of sex and marriage. Although it targets schools and youth groups, it also recently produced a presentation for parents to use with their pre-teens at home, in the hope of pre-empting much of the unhelpful stuff which is included in standard school sex education materials. The PowerPoint CD is available from the Lovewise office.

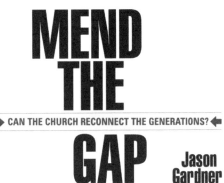

The familiar issues that create conflict between parents and children belie the rapid rate of cultural change surrounding family life. As society alters beyond recognition, the gap between young and old threatens to become a deep fracture in the heart of families, communities – and churches.

Urgent surgery is required to mend the gap.

Resisting simplistic solutions, Jason Gardner deftly analyses the reasons for the growing generation gap, including the role of the church. He provides practical steps forward for church leaders, youthworkers and parents. Underpinning this

hopeful book is an unshaking belief in Christ's burning ability to inspire a *'whole big, bad, beautiful mix of people to follow him, regardless of their age'.*

'A compelling insight into the challenges of creating and cherishing multi-generational church.'
Jill Rowe, Oasis UK Church

'I couldn't put this book down.'
Matt Summerfield, Urban Saints

'Born out of a deep concern, yet brimming with optimism, the pages of this book contain a wake-up call. Read it and act!'
Phil Green, Evangelical Alliance

ISBN:
978-1-84474-284-4

Available from your local Christian bookshop or via our website at **www.ivpbooks.com**

Married for God

making your marriage the best it can be

Christopher Ash

It seems rather obvious to look to our Maker for marriage instructions. After all, God invented marriage. Yet by nature we prefer to work it out for ourselves, starting with our own needs, hopes and desires.

This book turns our thinking upside down. The author examines the Bible's teaching on marriage, while remaining firmly earthed in the twenty-first-century world where messing up, heartbreak, divorce and sexual chaos are distressingly common. Starting with

God's grace applied to our pain and failure, the author centres on God's plan for sex and marriage, one of service.

'Refreshing, rigorous and readable. This book acts as a corrective to exaggerated claims and self-indulgent attitudes concerning wedlock endemic in our culture and becomes a call to joyful biblical simplicity and true God-centred liberty in marriage.'

John & Ann Benton

'An excellent, challenging and helpful book.' Martin & Elizabeth Goldsmith

ISBN:
978-1-84474-189-2

Available from your local Christian bookshop or via our website at **www.ivpbooks.com**

Books for older teens & students

'Dear friends, you are foreigners and strangers on this earth. So I beg you not to surrender to those desires that fight against you. Always let others see you behaving properly, even though they may still accuse you of doing wrong. Then on the day of judgment, they will honour God by telling the good things they saw you do.' **1 Peter 2:11-12**

Staying pure is a huge challenge to twenty-first-century young people, but with God's grace surely it's not impossible?

'Old habits die hard. We can be painfully aware of hypocrisy and failure, and tempted to give up. Yet the truth is that we have a new identity and a new destiny. At the heart of this identity is the call to purity. Pure will challenge you to lead a distinctive life. It will help you to avoid compromise, and make you excited about the opportunities and the adventure of a life well lived.'

Nigel Pollock
Director, Tertiary Students Christian
Fellowship, New Zealand

ISBN:
978-1-84474-090-1

Available from your local Christian bookshop
or via our website at **www.ivpbooks.com**

Books for older teens & students

bite-sized inspiration for students

Krish Kandiah

FRESH provides bite-sized daily inspirations and challenges for new students, covering everything from writing essays to writing home, from making friends to making the grade, from debt to dating.

FRESH offers a challenging introduction to maintaining a strong personal Christian faith but keeps its main emphasis on discovering how Christian students can make the most of their faith, relationships and studies.

An essential guide to keep the faith - FRESH is bursting with 5 weeks' worth of fresher-friendly ideas from someone who's been there and done that.

'Fresh gives new students tremendous biblical, gospel-centred and practical wisdom to help them navigate through their first few weeks of university. I would recommend it to any first year student.'

Tim Rudge, UCCF Field Director

ISBN:
978-1-84474-275-2

Available from your local Christian bookshop or via our website at **www.ivpbooks.com**

www.ivpbooks.com

For more details of books published by IVP, visit our website where you will find all the latest information, including:

Book extracts   Downloads
Author interviews   Online bookshop
Reviews   Christian bookshop finder

You can also sign up for our regular email newsletters, which are tailored to your particular interests, and tell others what you think about this book by posting a review.

We publish a wide range of books on various subjects including:

Christian living   Small-group resources
Key reference works   Topical issues
Bible commentary series   Theological studies